Untangling Leadership

Untangling Leadership

Aligning Mind and Heart to Advance Higher Education

Chris Heasley and Robert Palestini

ROWMAN & LITTLEFIELD
Lanham • Boulder • New York • London

Published by Rowman & Littlefield
An imprint of The Rowman & Littlefield Publishing Group, Inc.

4501 Forbes Boulevard, Suite 200, Lanham, Maryland 20706
www.rowman.com

86-90 Paul Street, London EC2A 4NE, United Kingdom

Copyright © 2023 by Christopher Heasley and Robert Palestini

All rights reserved. No part of this book may be reproduced in any form or by any electronic or mechanical means, including information storage and retrieval systems, without written permission from the publisher, except by a reviewer who may quote passages in a review.

British Library Cataloguing in Publication Information Available

Library of Congress Cataloging-in-Publication Data Available

ISBN 9781475861433 (cloth) | ISBN 9781475861440 (pbk.) | ISBN 9781475861457 (epub)

Dedication

To my girls, Addison, Cadence, and Rylan: your fierceness, kind hearts, and exploring minds continue to give hope for a bright future. Kristin, thank you for being my partner in life, for loving me, believing in me, supporting me, and pushing me to be a better person every day. And finally, to Bailey and Brooklyn, the cutest and laziest interns. Your unwavering companionship and loyalty provide comfort and happiness always.

Contents

Preface	ix
Acknowledgments	xi
Introduction	xiii
Chapter 1: Exploring Organizational Structure	1
Chapter 2: Nurturing Organizational Culture	7
Chapter 3: Applicable Leadership Theories and Conceptual Models	19
Chapter 4: Mindset for Motivational Change	33
Chapter 5: Effective Decision-Making	43
Chapter 6: Significance of Communication	57
Chapter 7: Managing Conflict	69
Chapter 8: Directing with Power	77
Chapter 9: Advancing with Strategy	83
Chapter 10: Leadership Through Transition	95
Chapter 11: Heart-Led Leadership	109
Chapter 12: Engaging the Material	117
Appendix: Heart Smart Surveys I and II	123
References	135
Index	141
About the Authors	143

Preface

Leaders who matter are effective agents of change in organizations. However, few are simply born into greatness; most leaders come to be through personal triumphs and tribulations, mentorship/sponsorship, and continued learning and practice. The latter is where this book finds its purpose.

Yet, providing a comprehensive, albeit direct, book about leadership in higher education is a challenging task. Nuanced peculiarities of each post-secondary institution, inconsistent position titles and responsibilities, and the ever-changing landscape of the educational market make authoring work about higher education (HE) leadership particularly formidable. Still, the need for resources remains.

Many books on this topic address leadership through a particular style or approach. Essentially, they begin at the end and impart only information. While this text provides an overview of the foundational principles and knowledge leaders need to be effective, this alone is insufficient to fully prepare future leaders. Aligning mind with heart integrates competency and skill development with emotional intelligence, empathy, kindness, and caring for others.

As HE administrators and leaders, *praxis*, applying theory to practice, is crucial for personal and professional growth. Yet, opportunities for practice may be limited to real-life scenarios, where risk is high and rewards are low. So, this text is crafted to be used as a workbook of sorts, providing case studies to help readers contextualize praxis in a simulated setting.

The hope is that this book will serve as a user manual—a go-to guide for HE leadership—and that it will quickly come to have torn edges, sticky notes protruding from the textblock, highlights and ink scribblings adorning its pages. We hope that it does more than collect dust on a shelf.

Acknowledgments

As always, a sincere thank you to Tom Koerner, whose continued support of our authorship is so appreciated. We also wish to thank all the staff at Rowman & Littlefield for their efforts in helping this book come to fruition. Lastly, to our department colleagues, we thank you for being a part of our continued learning and reflective process. Much of the content found within these pages came from our passionate and enlightening dialogue together.

Introduction

When creating an individualized organizational wellness plan, a pathway toward good health and growth, a process of deconstruction and reconstruction often takes place. With this process, one takes apart the whole in an effort to investigate its unique components. Only then, with new understanding and discoveries made, is the object rebuilt into something new using the same components.

This same approach serves as a guide for how this book was crafted. Specifically, each chapter addresses vital components of different organizational units (e.g., faculty departments, student-centered units, educational institutions). These topics speak to the so-called science of leadership but do not necessarily relate to the art of administration and leadership.

To fully understand *authentic* leadership in higher education, the roles assumed by the person, their mind, and their heart must be considered both separately and in relation to one another. Still, one must remember to lead with both mind (science) and heart (art) to be truly effective.

The authors contend that the effective building blocks of quality leadership are the skills of communication, motivation, organizational development, management, and creativity. Mastering theory and practice in these areas of study will produce high-quality leadership ability and, in turn, can produce successful leaders. Moreover, pairing leadership capacity and willingness with compassion (heart) not only results in highly successful leadership but also has the power to transcend into what some call heroic leadership (Lowney, 2003).

But how exactly does mastery of theory and practice work in tandem to ensure successful praxis? This is where deconstruction and reconstruction can be used as techniques of sensemaking and discovery. Suppose someone is working on a thousand-piece puzzle. By imagining the whole but working with the individual parts—parts composed of unique colors, patterns, shapes, and sizes—one can begin to build a recognizable image. Over time, and through reconstruction, the puzzle will become whole again.

Now imagine trying to solve a puzzle without knowing what image the pieces make. For many, such a task would be crippling. Faced with this proposition, most people would be unable to see the forest for the trees. Newly appointed, and not so newly appointed, administrators, faculty, and staff often have these same feelings of confusion when faced with the prospect of assuming a leadership role in a complex organization. Where does one start?

An effective way to address a complex task is to systematically examine the components that make up the organization. Such a process of organizational diagnosis and prescription leads to a comprehensive and integrated analysis of organizational strengths and weaknesses and points the way toward improvement.

This book provides a sequential and systematic approach by intentionally focusing on both the "trees" and the "forest." Found at the end of each chapter is a higher education case study. Readers should approach these activities with contemplative mindfulness as they determine a diagnosis (an explanation for the reasons for, or causes of, the behaviors and attitudes described in the case) and envision a prescription (an identified pathway or course of action for particular circumstances based on the foregoing diagnosis). Utilizing this learning strategy can effectively produce dramatic results toward leadership development.

Importantly, each chapter of this book is dedicated to one of the eleven essential components of an institution. Most of each chapter focuses on the implementation of these components, but there is some emphasis on the supporting theory that speaks to *why* these leadership practices are effective.

Readers are called to reflect on the brief case study found at the end of each chapter to more deeply consider the implications of practice. There is also a diagnostic debrief, a list of questions aimed at helping to quickly assess the status of these components in an educational organization and determine whether further work ought to be addressed.

In the appendices, there are two diagnostic instruments, Heart Smart Surveys I and II, that will help quantify the assessment process. For readers who are interested in exploring these topics as applied in a K-12 setting, a complementary sibling text entitled *Aligning Mind and Heart: Leadership and Organization Dynamics for Advancing K-12 Education* is highly recommended (Heasley & Palestini, 2022).

It is the authors' intention that by addressing questions of leadership and organizational change in a systematic and concrete way, readers can come to see *both* the forest and the trees and enable leading institutions to reach new heights (pun intended).

Chapter 1

Exploring Organizational Structure

> Leaders can create a high productivity level by providing the appropriate organizational structure and job design, and by acknowledging and appreciating hard work.
>
> —*A. P. J. Abdul Kalam*

There are three basic structures used to organize educational entities: the classical structure, the social systems structure, and the open systems structure. Despite being organized around one of these structures, most university systems and institutions of higher learning reflect certain aspects of each of these models (Heasley & Palestini, 2022). These structures are illustrated in **Figure 1.1.** The following sections of this chapter further detail each of these structures. Contingency theory is also presented as a contemporary model for organizational development.

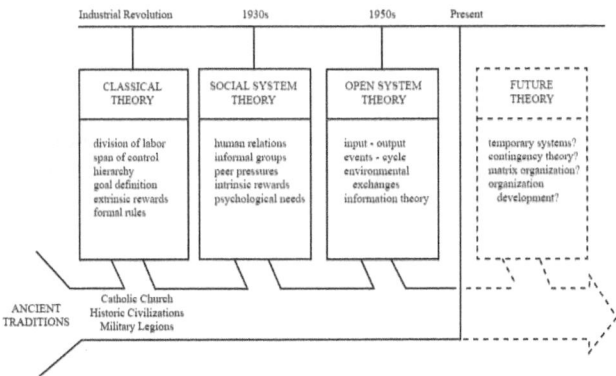

Figure 1.1. Organizational Theory and Structures

THE CLASSICAL THEORY

Classical theorists believe that the application of a bureaucratic structure and process will promote rational, efficient, and disciplined behavior, making possible the achievement of well-defined goals. Efficiency, then, is achieved by arranging positions and jurisdiction and by placing power at the top of a clear chain of command. The conceptual model of the classical theory has had a significant impact on education.

In higher educational settings, an institution's president often holds positional power at the top of the hierarchical structure of the organization. Trickling down from this post are the provost and operating officers, deans and department chairs, student affairs leaders, and eventually general faculty and staff personnel. Arguably, students comprise the lowest level of this structure. Virtually every educational system in the United States is organized according to the tenets of the classical theory.

Within the classical theory framework, the individual is conceived of as an object, a part of the bureaucratic machine (Weber, 1947). This is the antithesis of the second organizational theory, the social systems theory. Historically, researchers have found that the impact of social-psychological variables within the worker group is significant. The study of behavior in social systems settings intensified, and a greater sophistication developed about how and why group members behave as they do under given conditions. In time, a natural social systems orientation to the analysis of behavior evolved in the literature as an alternative to the rational or classical systems approach.

THE SOCIAL SYSTEMS THEORY

The conceptual perspective of the social systems model suggests an organization consists of a collection of groups (social systems) that collaborate to achieve system goals. Coalitions among subgroups within the organization (e.g., college of arts and sciences faculty, business faculty, education faculty) form to provide power bases upon which positive or negative action can be taken (e.g., "Let's all vote to accept general education core objectives."). As with the classical organizational theory, learning organizations and systems have been profoundly influenced by the social systems model.

THE OPEN SYSTEMS THEORY

A newer theory that is having a growing influence on educational institutions, especially higher education institutions, is the open systems model. The classical and social systems theories tend to view organizational life as a closed system—that is, as isolated from the surrounding environment. In contrast, open systems theory conceives of an organization as a set of interrelated parts that interact with the internal and external environments.

As an ecology-focused model, open systems theory receives "inputs" such as human and material resources, values, community expectations, and societal demands; transforms them through a production process (e.g., an educational program); and exports the product in the form of "outputs" (e.g., graduates, new knowledge, revised value sets) into the environment (e.g., businesses, the military, service providers) with "value added." The organization receives a return (e.g., community financial support in the form of taxes or tuition) for its efforts so it can survive and prosper. Then the cycle begins once again. **Figure 1.2** illustrates the open systems dynamic.

New logic on issues of organizational governance has emerged through the perspective of open systems theory. Within this system, practices emphasize the relationship of the organization to its surrounding environment and, thus, place a premium on planning and programming for events that cannot be controlled directly.

An organization's ability to gather, process, and utilize information is paramount to making an open system work effectively and efficiently. In an educational institution, then, the facility with which a need is discovered, a goal is established, and resources are coalesced to meet that need will determine the effectiveness and efficiency of that institution. Unlike businesses, educational institutions, especially colleges and universities, have not yet found a way to fully meet the demands of the open systems model.

CONTINGENCY THEORY

In more contemporary times, a view of organizational development has surfaced that treats each organization, and even the entities within the organization, as relatively unique. For centuries, this orientation has been at the core of practitioner behavior, but it has been seen as an anomaly, reflective of inefficiency or unpreparedness, and thus overlooked by management scientists. Currently, the changing situational character of management is coming to be understood as a key to the management process itself.

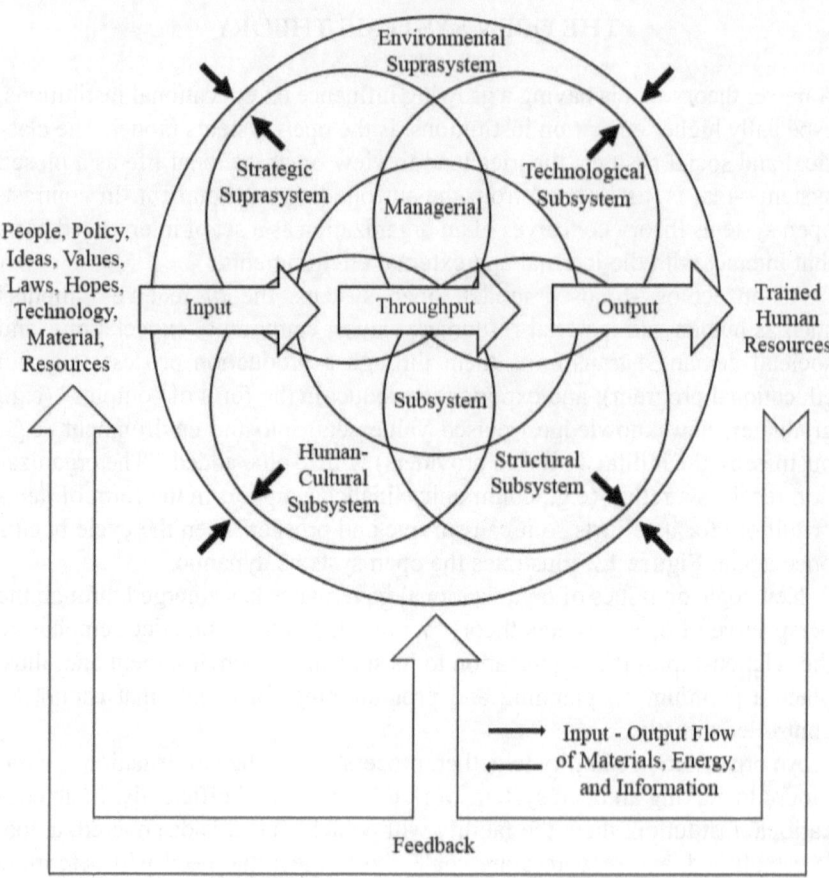

Many management scholars and practitioners agree with the observation that contingency theory is perhaps the most powerful current and future trend in the organizational field. At this stage of development, however, contingency theory is not really a theory. Rather, it is a conceptual tool that facilitates understanding of the situational flow of events and alternate organizational and individual responses to that flow.

As a conceptual tool, contingency theory does not possess the holistic character of the three major models discussed earlier. In many ways, contingency theory can be thought of as a subset of open systems theory because it is through open systems theory that one comes to understand the dynamic flows of events, personnel, and resources that take place in organizations.

In any case, the implication of contingency theory is that institutions should employ the best of all three theoretical models—classical, social systems, and open systems—depending on the situation or context in order to have a maximally effective organizational structure. Thus, a contingency organizational structure can be described as an institutional *mindset* rather than as an organizational chart, since, unlike the classical theory, it is difficult to depict the attributes of social systems and open systems theory in the form of an organizational chart.

As a preview of coming attractions, this book will incorporate contingency theory thinking in discussions of leadership, employee motivation, communication, decision-making, conflict resolution, and many other components of an organization.

IMPLICATIONS FOR PRACTICE: EXPLORING ORGANIZATIONAL STRUCTURE CASE STUDY

Grand View College (GVC) is a small, suburban, four-year institution of higher learning with an undergraduate population of 1,500 students. Contrary to the dictates of classical organizational structure, many of the administrators and faculty play dual roles, necessitated by insufficient resources and funding. The college houses two competing schools: humanities and business.

Within the last two decades, the distribution of majors has steadily shifted so that the current proportion of students majoring in business is nearly 60 percent of the total undergraduate population. As a result, there is much competition between the schools in terms of academic prestige, faculty compensation, and learning resources.

The GVC board of trustees recently voted against approval of next year's university budget. This decision was made despite better structure and improvement management systems presented in the proposed budget. An article in *The Chronicle of Higher Education* featured the budget defeat, citing tensions between faculty and administration. The GVC president was quoted as accepting blame for the budget defeat, stating, "The defeat suggests I was unable to adequately articulate the reasons for the requested funding for staff/faculty structural adjustments and merit pay increases." The article further cited declining enrollment, lack of athletic prominence, and low alumni support as factors contributing to this recent budgeting decision.

A negative vote was foreseeable. When asked, several trustee members said they voted "no" because they didn't want to reward low enrollment numbers. As a result of the defeat, greatly needed and anticipated budget increases for restructuring compensation were denied. University administrators, faculty, and staff remained overburdened, and many leaders were asked to take on even more tasks and oversight for their areas of responsibility with no additional pay or resources. In addition, as disgruntled administrators and staff resigned, their positions were not filled, thus causing increased workloads for those who remained. Employee morale was at an all-time low.

Programs were also negatively impacted by the denied budget vote. Academic and bridge programs were reviewed to be cut. For example, funding for the summer STEM preparation program for incoming first-year students matriculating from underserved and under-resourced high schools was cut by 30 percent. This was a pilot program that had gained favorable attention from worthy news outlets the year prior. Varsity and club sports teams were also reviewed. Many teams with low winning records were in jeopardy of being cut.

DIAGNOSTIC DEBRIEF

Here are some questions to consider when assessing an institution's organizational structure:

- Are the best aspects of the classical, social systems, and open systems organizational structures present?
- Is there appropriate division of labor, and is it flexible?
- Is the division of labor conducive to reaching organizational goals?
- Is the structure of the organization well designed?
- Is there a respect for human dignity in the organization?
- Does the organization's structure respond to environmental contingencies?

Chapter 2

Nurturing Organizational Culture

> Your culture is a combination of what you create and what you allow.
>
> —*Craig Groeschel*

Much can be said about organizational culture. It is the epitome of values in action. When properly nurtured, it can help move the whole organization forward, keeping employees motivated and providing synergy for future direction and success. Conversely, when organizational culture is neglected, it can negatively affect the entire workforce, ceasing meaningful work productivity and potentially leading to a toxic organizational environment.

The astute administrator will become familiar with the territory in their educational institution. Knowing the landscape in education translates into being keenly aware of organizational structure and culture. Understanding how one's educational entity is structured within the context of the three models described in chapter 1 (classical, social systems, and open systems) is the first step in an educational leader's quest to truly "know the territory."

The second step in navigating a new institutional system is to be aware of the institution's organizational behavior or culture. Organizational culture is composed of the shared beliefs, expectations, values, and norms of conduct of its members. In any organization, the informal culture interacts with the formal structure and control system to produce a generally clear understanding of "the way things are done around here." Even more than the forces of bureaucracy, the organization's culture binds people together or tears them apart (Delmestri & Goodrick, 2016).

Anyone who has visited a number of educational institutions develops a sense of their different "personalities" or cultures. Walking the hallways and campus of an educational institution, a keen observer can see physical manifestations of an underlying set of values: perhaps religious iconography across campus; classroom desks bolted to the floor; clean and well-maintained grounds; an oversized football stadium and athletic prominence that overshadows academic curriculum; clandestine meetings between school leaders, students, or faculty; and so forth.

Based on myriad external observations, institutions of higher education have been alternately characterized as money-hungry machines, professional athlete training grounds, diploma mills, Ivy League institutions, contributors to democracy, purveyors of academic freedom, and more. Still, why are the views of higher education so varied?

The aforementioned are tangible aspects of an institution's culture. The intangible aspects often parallel those values. Colleges and universities often attempt to develop shared values and enculturate them using symbols, mottos, mascots, and chants at athletic events. Other symbols of an organization's culture are the heroes and storytellers, faculty members and/or administrators who have earned legendary status.

Administrators can influence the institution's culture in a positive way. First, however, they must be aware of its importance and its components. If the educational leader has a thorough knowledge of the institution's culture, they can set about trying to influence it. One way of doing so is to take time each day to review this and the nine other "secrets" to effective institutional management presented in this book.

Ultimately, the best way to influence the institution's culture is by modeling desired behavior. If the leaders want the faculty and staff to be efficient and effective, the leaders need to manifest those same characteristics in their own behavior. However, none of these desired changes will occur unless a culture of mutual trust and respect has been established.

THE PROCESSES OF ORGANIZATIONAL CULTURE

Next begins an exploration of areas of organizational culture that deal with the way leaders perceive events or other people; the way they understand the events and people; the way past experiences and acquisition of knowledge and information influence this description and diagnosis; and the way leaders form attitudes about the situations based on their perceptions, understanding, and experience. These four processes are referred to as perception, attribution, learning, and attitude formation. Understanding them greatly enhances an administrator's ability to influence the school's culture.

Perception

Perception is the process by which each person discerns reality and comes to a particular understanding or view. It is an active process that results in different people having somewhat different, even contradictory, views or understandings of the same event or person. Rarely do different observers describe events or persons in exactly the same way. Often, administrators and their subordinates, coworkers, or supervisors see and describe the same situation differently.

Perceptual Distortions

Perceptions sometimes suffer from inaccuracies or distortions. Although such biases are normal and human, they can have significant consequences when administrators or other members of the institution base their actions on potentially invalid distortions. This chapter discusses stereotyping, the halo effect, projection, and the self-fulfilling prophecy as examples.

Stereotyping

When an individual attributes behaviors or attitudes to a person on the basis of the group or category to which that person belongs, *stereotyping* occurs. An example of a stereotype would be "Low-income students aren't as smart as affluent students." Frequently, stereotypes are based on social identity categorizations such as ethnicity, socioeconomic status, gender, religion, place of origin, or positions of power (e.g., administrators, faculty, support personnel).

Why does stereotyping occur? Often individuals do not gather sufficient data about others to describe their behaviors or attitudes accurately. They may look for shortcuts to describe certain phenomenon without taking the time to analyze them completely. Alternatively, some individuals have personal biases (both explicit and implicit) against certain groups of individuals (we will discuss this in more detail later in this chapter).

Historical attitudes toward certain cultural groups may result in stereotypes. Americans may have certain views of Europeans and different views of Japanese people based on their historical experiences with the two groups. Using stereotypes reduces the accuracy of perceptions about others.

The Halo Effect

The *halo effect* refers to an individual letting one salient feature of a person dominate the evaluation of that individual. A faculty member who volunteers for extra projects, for example, might be evaluated by a department chair as highly competent and effective in the classroom. A neat personal appearance can cause a person to be judged as being precise in their work and well organized.

The halo effect frequently occurs in assessments of faculty and staff performance. Individuals may be judged on the basis of one trait—for example, promptness, neatness, or enthusiasm—rather than on a composite of traits and skills observed over a period of time (Heilman & Stopeck, 1985).

Projection

You may have heard coworkers saying such things as, "My supervisor is prejudiced," "My director is just intimidated by a strong personality," or "The residence life coordinator doesn't like people from underserved communities." These observations about administrators may be accurate, but they may also reflect prejudices.

Consider an admissions counselor who hesitantly approaches a prospective student's parent, worried that the parent will think the school is unable to offer a quality education to their child. The counselor may be seeing their own attitudes or feelings about the institution in the parent's response, whether or not the parent actually has similar thoughts.

Projection refers to an individual attributing their own attitudes or feelings to another person. Individuals use projection as a defense mechanism, to transfer blame to another person, or to provide protection from their own unacceptable feelings.

Individuals frequently attribute their own prejudices against members of marginalized communities, supervisors, or employees, for example, to another party. Hence, projection and its dysfunctional consequences can increase as the workforce becomes more diverse; individuals who lack understanding or mistrust people who are different from themselves may project these insecurities onto others.

Self-Fulfilling Prophecy

In many situations, individuals expect certain behaviors from other individuals or groups. They then see these behaviors as occurring whether or not they actually do. In such cases, their expectations become *self-fulfilling prophecies*. For example, someone may expect workers to be lazy, bossy, or tardy; then they perceive that these people actually are lazy, bossy, or tardy. These expectations may be associated with stereotyping, the halo effect, or projection.

Perceptions of others can be influenced by bias and inaccurate assumptions, and these perceptions have been shown to influence the performance of those for whom expectations exist. For example, many studies link faculty expectations and student achievement. If an instructor expects an underserved student to fail, the student is more likely to fail. Conversely, if an instructor expects all students to achieve, they are more likely to achieve.

Instances of self-fulfilling prophecy are not limited to one-on-one circumstances. For example, if employees think their unit or department within a college or university is going to close as part of a reorganization plan, the self-fulfilling prophecy often takes effect and staff morale and performance decline, leading to the actual closing of the unit or department. Here, thoughts influence behaviors and outcomes.

Dealing with Distortions

How can dysfunctional perceptual distortions in organizations be reduced?

1. Individuals must gather sufficient information about other people's behavior and attitudes to encourage more realistic perceptions. Administrators, for example, must judge an individual's performance on their observed behavior rather than on the behavior of a group to which the person belongs.
2. Administrators must check their conclusions to ensure their validity. This includes being aware of explicit and implicit biases (these terms are explained later in this chapter).
3. Members of the organization must differentiate between facts and assumptions in determining the basis of their perceptions. This work has no end and ought to be omnipresent in the workplace.
4. Individuals must distinguish among various aspects of an individual's behavior rather than grouping even superficially related aspects. More specifically, they must separate appearance from performance, productivity from attendance, and personality from creativity.
5. To eliminate or reduce projection, individuals must first identify their true feelings. Do they feel anger, uncertainty, and mistrust? After recognizing these feelings, administrators must repeatedly assess whether and how these feelings are influencing their perceptions of others.

The Attribution Process

It is a basic human need to try to figure out why things happen the way they do. It is inherent in the diagnostic approach good administrators often take toward problem solving. Consciously, it seems most prudent to first ponder the reasons for an event and then decide why the event occurred. In this way, one attributes a cause to an event. This process leads to a movement from description to diagnosis. This is the process simulated in the case studies found at the end of each chapter of this text. Still, as might be expected, different people often attribute a different cause to the same event.

Attribution theorists and researchers have studied the process of determining the causes of specific events, the responsibility for particular outcomes, and the personal qualities of individuals participating in the situation. For example, a department chair might deduce that a decline in an instructor's teaching performance is due to the introduction of a new curriculum; if so, the poor performance will be attributed to situational factors. If, however, the instructor is perceived as lazy or inept, then a leader is likely to conclude that the instructor's personal disposition caused the change.

Although both situational and personal factors may have influenced the change in performance, people in leadership roles often oversimplify a situation and attend primarily to only one cause.

Attribution and Locus of Control

Attribution and the concept of locus of control are closely related. Locus of control is the feeling an individual has about whether they are in control of their own destiny. Whether one believes that internal or external factors affect future events determines whether one has an internal or external locus of control. Those with an internal locus of control believe that future events are determined by their own individual abilities and personal qualities, while those with an external locus of control attribute future outcomes to factors outside of their control.

Thus, the student who attributes their poor performance on a test to the faculty's inability to teach the subject in a meaningful way can be said to have an external locus of control, while the student who attributes their poor performance to their own lack of preparation would tend to have an internal locus of control. The objective for educational leaders, then, would be to develop a strong internal locus of control in both themselves and their staff members (Chen & Leung, 2016).

The Learning Process

Learning refers to the acquisition of skills, knowledge, abilities, or attitudes, and it influences the organizational culture of an educational institution. As with perception and attribution, there are complexities to the learning process. The section that follows focuses on the ways individuals learn, beginning with three models of learning and concluding with the administrative implications of learning.

The Behaviorist Approach

Behaviorists emphasize external influences and the power of rewards in learning, as well as the link between a given stimulus and response. For instance, in classical conditioning, after repeated pairing of neutral and unconditioned stimuli, solitary presentation of the neutral stimulus leads to a conditioned response (Thorndike, 1924).

Recall Pavlov's groundbreaking work with dogs, still used as a seminal case for explaining the behaviorist approach to learning. He noted that upon presentation of powdered meat blown through a tube (unconditioned stimulus), the dog salivated (unconditioned response). The ringing of a bell (neutral stimulus) yielded no salivation response. After pairing the ringing bell with the meat several times, Pavlov then rang the bell without the meat, and the dog salivated (conditioned response) (Pavlov, 1927).

Operant conditioning extends classical conditioning to focus on the consequences of a behavior. While a stimulus can still cue a response behavior, the desired or undesired consequence that follows the behavior determines whether the behavior will recur. For example, an individual who receives a bonus (a positive consequence) after creative performance (behavior) on a work assignment (stimulus) is more likely to repeat the creative behavior than if their performance is ignored (a negative consequence).

The Cognitive Approach

In contrast to the behavior reinforcement links central to behaviorist theories, cognitive theorists emphasize the internal mental processes involved in gaining new insights. They view learning as occurring from the joining of various cues in the environment into a mental map. In early cognitive experiments, rats learned to run through a maze to reach a food goal. Repeated trials caused the rats to develop and strengthen cognitive connections, thereby identifying the correct pathway to the goal (Tolman, 1932).

Employees, too, can develop a cognitive map that shows the path to a specific outcome. In this case, the cognitive processes join the stimulus to result in a given behavior. On-the-job training, like a new employee induction process, should result in a new cognitive map of job performance for new team members.

The Social Learning Approach

Extending beyond both behavioral and cognitive learning theories, social learning theory integrates the behaviorist and cognitive approaches with the idea of modeling or imitating behaviors. Learners first watch others who act as models, next develop a mental picture of the behavior and its consequences, and finally try the behavior. If positive consequences result, the learner repeats the behavior; if negative consequences occur, the learner likely will not repeat the behavior.

The learning impact occurs when the subject tries the behavior and experiences a favorable result, as in the behaviorist approach. At the same time, the learner's development of a cognitive image of the situation incorporates a basic aspect of cognitive learning. The need for educational leaders to act as exemplars, taking responsibility for their actions, is paramount in social learning environments. In addition, administrators need to model the behavior they expect of the staff and faculty (Bandura, 1978; Balch et al., 2021).

Implicit and Explicit Bias

Everyone has biases, or preconceived notions about others, and there are many bias types that may elicit a positive or negative thought or response. Of particular interest is whether one is aware of such thoughts and how one responds or acts based on them.

Explicit bias describes the conscious attitudes and beliefs held about a person or group. In some cases, such biases and their expression may arise as the direct result of a perceived threat. Implicit or unconscious bias operates outside of the person's awareness. Interestingly, for some people, implicit bias may be contradictory to their espoused beliefs and values.

Unconscious bias can also lead to unintended consequences. Functioning like autocorrect in a texting app, implicit bias can automatically, and without the person's full awareness, influence their affect or behavior. Implicit bias can be subcategorized into several types, such as gender bias, racial bias, conformity bias, and halo effect.

Cultural Competency in the Learning Space

There are multiple models, theories, and assessments that seek to illustrate, explain, and measure cultural competency. Put simply, cultural competency is the ability to understand and effectively communicate across categories of cultural difference. Examples of cultural competency might include a teacher speaking about the negative consequences of settler colonialism and its effect on white centeredness; including in literature study, books that positively illustrate children being raised by same-gender parents; or developing curriculum using a variety of textbooks written by both white and non-white authors.

Being culturally competent extends beyond attending a one-time professional development experience or being friends with those different from yourself. Conceptually, developing cultural competency is a constant exercise in understanding and honoring difference. Exposure to varied histories, cultures, languages, traditions, and religious practices are all components that impact one's level of cultural competency (Engle & Gonzales, 2014).

Being valued matters. Acknowledging individual differences, capacities, and abilities by showing respect, humility, kindness, and curiosity helps increase cultural competency awareness and skill development for both school leaders and students. Current scholars further posit that leaders with high cultural competency demonstrate culturally responsive practices. Such practices recognize and incorporate the skills, assets, and strengths of all members of the organization (Williams, 2018).

The policies, procedures, and practices of a culturally responsive educational organization ensure that learning experiences are relevant to all students and that learning outcomes, instruction, and assessment are aligned to safeguard against exclusionary practices.

Managerial Implications of Learning

How can school administrators encourage their own and others' learning in the workplace? They can ensure that appropriate conditions for learning exist; providing appropriate stimuli (e.g., professional development materials) should facilitate acquisition of the desired skills or attitudes.

Administrators should reinforce desired learned behaviors. They should also provide environmental cues that encourage learning; structuring a context that supports learning is essential. In effect, just as leaders advise faculty to adapt their teaching styles to the variety of learning styles of their students, administrators must adapt their management styles to the variety of learning styles that are present among their faculty members.

Administrators can use a modeling strategy for success. For instance, an administrator could identify the goal or target behaviors that will lead to improved performance. After selecting the appropriate model, the administrator must determine whether to present the model through a live demonstration, video recording, other media, or a combination of all these. Next, the administrator would ensure teachers are capable of meeting the technical skill requirements of the target behavior. As a result of learning the new skill, a more extensive use of cooperative learning activities might lead to improving students' social skills.

If in the aforementioned scenario further change is deemed necessary, the administrator must structure a favorable and positive learning environment to increase the likelihood that the teachers will learn the new behavior and act in the desired way. Starting cooperative learning with a particularly skilled teacher and a cooperative group of students will ensure success.

Administrators must also model the target behavior and carry out supporting activities, such as role playing. Conducting a faculty meeting using cooperative learning techniques would be an example of such a strategy.

Continued practice leads to continued success. Administrators should positively reinforce reproduction of the target behaviors both in training and in the workplace. Teacher-of-the-month awards are an example of this strategy. Once the target behaviors are reproduced, administrators must maintain and strengthen them through a system of rewards until the behavior is institutionalized—that is, it becomes part of the institutional culture.

In summation, then, administrators need to model a desired behavior and then reward it when it occurs. As a result, educational institutions will become learning organizations (Alagaraja & Herd, 2022; Senge, 1990).

Developing Positive Attitudes

Attitude formation is another aspect of organizational behavior and culture. An attitude is a consistent predisposition to respond to various aspects of people, situations, or objects. An attitude is also a response to a person's behavior or expressed attitude, as well as from other cognitive, affective, or connotative responses.

Attitudes are pervasive and predict behavior toward their objects. For example, a leader might determine an individual's level of job satisfaction by inferring it from the employee's general demeanor on the job or by asking the person to describe this attitude.

Data can be formally and informally collected to support claims. Attitude surveys or other collections of attitude scales to assess individuals' attitudes toward their job, coworkers, supervisor, or the school or school system at large are often used in this way. Once again, being a change agent helps in developing an overall positive attitude within an educational institution.

IMPLICATIONS FOR PRACTICE: NURTURING ORGANIZATIONAL CULTURE CASE STUDY

Dr. Melissa Johnson is a junior tenure-track faculty member at Webber University, a predominantly white institution on the east coast of the United States. Dr. Johnson is approaching her mid-tenure review, nearing the end of her three years in the finance department.

To assist her in this process, a colleague who passed their mid-tenure review a few years prior shares their submission materials. As she reviews her colleague's submission, Dr. Johnson realizes there are significant differences in workload distribution. As the only faculty member of color in the finance department and only one of three in the entire school of business, Dr. Johnson feels it is necessary to approach her department chair to speak about the inequity in the number of student advisees divided among the faculty in the department and the number of course preps requested by junior faculty each semester.

First, the chair looks at the roster of students within the department and retorts that each faculty member has roughly fifty-five to sixty-five students to advise, and therefore he does not understand this raised concern. Dr. Johnson explains that many of the students of color in the school of business seek her out as an academic adviser even when the student is assigned to a different faculty member in the department.

The chair merely says, "Well, stop seeing students who aren't assigned to you. There, problem fixed! As for course preps, senior faculty get first pick of the days and times they want to instruct. They also get first pick of courses they want to teach. It just so happens this has prevented you from teaching the same course more than once a semester. I'm not going to apologize for the privileges that come with being tenured."

DIAGNOSTIC DEBRIEF

Here are some questions that can assess an institution's organizational culture:

- Does the organization exhibit a culture of mutual trust and respect?
- Do perceptual distortions proliferate?
- Does the workforce exhibit an internal locus of control?
- Is the institution a learning organization?
- Are the various learning styles being addressed in the management process?
- Is the leader adapting their leadership style to the learning style of the followers?
- What beliefs and values do the individuals in the organization have?
- How do these beliefs and values influence individual attitudes?
- What functional and dysfunctional behaviors result from the individuals' perceptions, attributions, learning, and attitudes?
- Are the leaders modeling desired behavior?

Chapter 3

Applicable Leadership Theories and Conceptual Models

> Presenting leadership as a list of carefully defined qualities (like strategic, analytic, and performance-oriented) no longer holds. Instead, true leadership stems from individuality that is honestly and sometimes imperfectly expressed. Leaders should strive for authenticity over perfection.
>
> —*Sheryl Sandberg*

Offered as a solution to most of the problems of organizations everywhere, leadership is often given credit for an organization's success and the blame for its demise. Institutions will work, it is often said, if presidents, provosts, deans, faculty, administrators, and staff provide strong instructional leadership. Organizations will be successful if they have visionary leaders. Around the world, administrators and managers say that their organizations would thrive if only senior management would provide strategy, vision, and real leadership. Though the call for leadership is universal, there is much less clarity about what the term means, especially in times of lingering uncertainty.

Historically, researchers in this scholarly field have searched for the best leadership style that would be most effective in all cases. The current prevailing thought, however, is there is no perfect style—that is, one size does not fit all. Rather, a combination of styles depending on the situation in which the leader finds themselves has been found to be more appropriate (Kirkpatrick & Locke, 1991). To understand the evolution of leadership theory, this chapter takes a historical approach and traces the progress of leadership theory beginning with the trait perspective of leadership and moving to the more current contingency theories of leadership.

TRAIT THEORY

The belief that an individual possesses certain personality traits, social traits, and physical characteristics, and can then evaluate leadership and propose ways of leading effectively, supports *trait theory*. Popular in the 1940s and 1950s, trait theory attempts to predict which individuals will become successful leaders and whether they will be effective in this role. It was suggested that leaders differ from non-leaders in their drive, desire to lead, honesty and integrity, self-confidence, cognitive ability, and knowledge of their field.

Limitations in the ability of traits to predict effective leadership caused researchers during the 1950s to view a person's *behavior* rather than their personal traits as more indicative of their leadership effectiveness. This view also paved the way for later behavioral and situational theories.

The types of leadership behaviors investigated typically fell into two categories: production oriented and employee oriented. Production-oriented leadership, also called concern for production, initiating structure, or task-focused leadership, involves acting primarily to get the task done. An administrator who tells their biology department chair to "do everything they need to do to get the new ecology curriculum developed on time for the start of the academic semester, regardless of the personal consequences" demonstrates production-oriented leadership. The same is true for an administrator who uses an autocratic style or fails to involve workers in any aspect of decision-making.

Employee-oriented leadership, also referred to as a concern for people or collaborative leadership, focuses on supporting individual workers in their activities and involving workers in decision-making. A dean of students who demonstrates great concern for their staff members' job satisfaction and is sensitive to both their personal and professional needs has an employee-oriented leadership style.

SITUATIONAL LEADERSHIP THEORY

Contingency or situational models differ from the earlier trait and behavioral models in asserting that no single way of leading works in all situations. Rather, appropriate behavior depends on the circumstances at a given time. Effective managers diagnose the situation, identify the leadership style that will be most effective, and then determine whether they can implement the required style (Meier, 2016).

Research suggests that the effect of leadership behaviors on performance is altered by such intervening variables as the effort of subordinates, their ability to perform their jobs, the clarity of their job responsibilities, the organization of the work, the cooperation and cohesiveness of the group, the sufficiency of resources and support provided to the group, and the coordination of work group activities with those of other subunits. Thus, leaders must respond to these and broader cultural differences in choosing an appropriate style.

THE BOLMAN/DEAL MODEL

Bolman and Deal have developed a unique situational leadership theory that analyzes leadership behavior through four frames of reference: structural, human resource, political, and symbolic. Each of the frames offers a different perspective on what leadership is and how it operates in organizations. Each can result in either effective or ineffective conceptions of leadership (Bolman & Deal, 1991).

Structural leaders develop a new model of the relationships among structure, strategy, and environment for their organizations. They focus on implementation. The right answer helps only if it can be implemented. They are often referred to by their followers as direct, no-nonsense, and hands-on managers.

Structural leaders sometimes fail because they miscalculate the difficulty of putting their design into action. They often underestimate the resistance that it will generate, and they take few steps to build a base of support for their innovations. In short, they are often undone by human resource, political, and symbolic considerations. Structural leaders do continually experiment, evaluate, and adapt, but because they fail to consider the entire environment in which they are situated, they are sometimes ineffective.

Human resource leaders believe in people and communicate that belief. They are passionate about "productivity through people." They demonstrate this faith in their words and actions and often build it into a philosophy or credo that is central to their vision of their organization. Human resource leaders are visible and accessible. Peters and Waterman (1988) popularized the notion of "management wandering around"—the idea that managers need to get out of their offices and interact with workers and customers. Many educational administrators have adopted this management principle.

Effective human resource leaders empower—that is, they increase participation, provide support, share information, and move decision-making as far down the organization as possible. Human resource leaders often like to refer to their employees as "partners" or "colleagues." They want to make it clear that employees have a stake in the organization's success and a right to be involved in making decisions. When this type of leader is ineffective, however, they are seen as naive or as a weakling or wimp.

Political leaders clarify what they want and what they can get. Political leaders are realists above all. They never let what they want cloud their judgment about what is possible. They assess the distribution of power and interests.

The political leader needs to think carefully about the players, their interests, and their power; in other words, the leader must map the political terrain. Political leaders ask questions such as, Whose support do I need? How do I go about getting it? Who are my opponents? How much power do they have? What can I do to reduce the opposition? Is the battle winnable? However, if ineffective, these leaders are perceived as being untrustworthy and manipulative.

The symbolic frame provides a fourth turn of the kaleidoscope of leadership. In this frame, the organization is seen as a stage, a theater in which every actor plays certain roles and attempts to communicate the right impressions to the right audiences. The main premise of this frame is that whenever reason and analysis fail to contain the dark forces of ambiguity, human beings erect symbols, myths, rituals, and ceremonies to bring order, meaning, and predictability out of chaos and confusion.

Transforming leaders are visionary leaders, and visionary leadership is invariably symbolic. Examination of symbolic leaders reveals that they follow a consistent set of practices and rules. Transforming leaders use symbols to capture attention.

For example, consider a newly appointed, first-time college president who knows they will face a substantial challenge. The school has all the usual problems of a rural public institution: decaying physical plant, lack of student scholarships, racial tension, troubles securing and retaining quality faculty, low employee morale, and limited resources. The only good news is that the situation is so bad, almost any change would be an improvement. In this situation, symbolic leaders will try to do something visible, even dramatic, to let people know that changes are on the way. Consider what would happen if (during the summer before they assumed their duties), this president wrote a letter to every department leader to set up an individual meeting. What if they traveled to meet department leaders wherever they wanted, even if it meant driving two hours? And what if, when meeting with staff, the president engaged in meaningful dialogue, asking the department leaders how they feel about the institution and what changes they want?

Building on the scenario, consider the president also feels that something needs to be done about the dilapidated state of the physical facilities. In response, they decide to have the front doors on the hallmark campus building on the campus green and some of the worst classrooms repainted. They have no delusions about the challenges they will face getting through the bureaucracy of securing contractors for this job scope, so they persuade some local families, alumni, and community members to help paint. When the college reopens, students and employees immediately see that things are going to be different, if only symbolically. Perhaps even more important, faculty, staff, and administrators receive a subtle challenge to contribute themselves.

Moral framing can be used to view situational leadership theory and the Bolman/Deal model in tandem. Here, the moral frame completes situational leadership theory. Without it, leaders could just as easily use their leadership skills to promote evil as to promote good. Leaders operating out of the moral frame are concerned about their obligations to their followers.

Moral frame leaders use some type of moral compass to direct their behavior. They practice what has been described as servant leadership and are concerned with those individuals and groups that are marginalized in their organizations and in society. In short, they are concerned about equality, fairness, and social justice. The moral frame is explored in more detail in chapter 11 (Heasley & Palestini, 2022).

Leadership Behaviors

Lest one be confused about what leadership behaviors fit into what frames, here are some examples:

Structural Frame Behaviors

- Developing a vision
- Setting goals
- Developing a strategic plan
- Implementing the plan
- Proposing and implementing change in the form of improvements
- Supervising followers closely
- Developing rules and regulations
- Developing job descriptions and responsibilities
- Striving for the magis (continuous improvement, seeking and reaching for more/greater)
- Demonstrating competency (knowledgeable, organized, industrious, passionate, committed)
- Managing using a hands-on style
- Attending to detail
- Being a lifelong learner
- Preparing meticulously
- Behaving authoritatively
- Using analytical and logical thinking
- Mastering the technical aspects of one's profession

Human Resource Frame Behaviors

- Developing a system of rewards to motivate employees
- Giving praise for accomplishments
- Empowering others
- Showing concern for the individual, the whole person (*cura personalis*)
- Making decisions using a participative model
- Building a team
- Acknowledging special occasions (e.g., birthdays, anniversaries, get-well sentiments)
- Managing by walking around (being visible)

Symbolic Frame Behaviors

- Showing concern for one's personal appearance
- Modeling desired behavior
- Giving motivational speeches and writing motivational publications
- Displaying inspirational quotes, slogans, adages (e.g., on letterhead, posters)
- Displaying symbols of achievement in the workplace
- Telling stories and jokes
- Being visible

Political Frame Behaviors

- Negotiating a contract or covenant on compensation and working conditions
- Lobbying for improvements
- Raising funds and providing institutional development activities
- Making compromises (*quid pro quo*)
- Building political and social capital
- Engaging in force field analysis (neutralizing opposing forces) to effect change

Moral Frame Behaviors

- Developing a personal moral compass to guide one's behavior
- Striving for the magis (the greater good, striving for excellence)
- Modeling personal integrity and moral character (being honest and forthright)
- Being sensitive to the human needs of all (*cura personalis*), especially the marginalized in the workplace

- Being concerned about equality, fairness, and social justice in the workplace and in society

THE HERSEY/BLANCHARD MODEL

In an attempt to integrate previous knowledge about leadership into a prescriptive model of leadership style, this model cites the "readiness of followers," defined as their ability and willingness to accomplish a specific task, as the major contingency that influences appropriate leadership style (Hersey & Blanchard, 1979; 1988; 1996).

Follower readiness incorporates the follower's level of achievement motivation, ability, and willingness to assume responsibility for their own behavior in accomplishing specific tasks, and education and experience relevant to the task. The model combines task and relationship behavior to yield four possible styles, as shown in **Figure 3.1**.

Leaders should use a telling style, and provide specific instructions and closely supervise performance, when followers are unable and unwilling

Leader Behavior

Readiness Level III Participating Style	Readiness Level II Selling Style
Readiness Level IV Delegating Style	Readiness Level I Telling Style

Follower Readiness

Level IV	Level III	Level II	Level I
seasoned veteran and/or very secure	much experience and/or secure	some experience and/or confidence	inexperienced and/or insecure

Figure 3.1. Readiness of Followers Model

or insecure (R1). Leaders should use a selling style, and explain decisions and provide opportunity for clarification, when followers have moderate to low readiness (R2). Leaders should use a participating style, where they share ideas and facilitate decision-making, when followers have moderate to high readiness (R3). Finally, leaders should use a delegating style, and give responsibility for decisions and implementation to followers, when followers are able, willing, and confident (R4).

Although some researchers have questioned the conceptual clarity, validity, robustness, and utility of the model, as well as the instruments used to measure leadership style, others have supported the utility of the theory. For example, the Leadership Effectiveness and Description Scale and related instruments, developed to measure leadership style by Hersey and Blanchard, continue to be widely used in industrial training programs. This model can easily be adapted to educational administration and used analytically to understand leadership deficiencies and to prescribe the appropriate style for a variety of situations.

TRANSFORMATIONAL LEADERSHIP

Transformational leaders are situational but are also able to use their personal charisma to inspire their followers. They talk to their followers about how essential their performance is, how confident they are in the followers, how exceptional the followers are, and how they expect the group's performance to exceed expectations (Anderson, 2017).

Barack Obama, Warren Buffett, Jack Welsh, and Bill Gates in industry, and Marie Montessori, Marcus Foster, and former Notre Dame president Reverend Theodore Hesburgh in education are examples of transformational leaders. Such leaders use dominance, self-confidence, a need for influence, and conviction of moral righteousness to increase their charisma and consequently their leadership effectiveness.

By recognizing an opportunity and developing a vision, communicating that vision to organizational members, building trust in the vision, and achieving the vision by motivating organizational members, a transformational leader changes an organization. The leader helps subordinates recognize the need to revitalize the organization by developing a felt need for change, overcoming resistance to change, and avoiding quick-fix solutions to problems.

Encouraging subordinates to act as devil's advocates with regard to the leader, building networks outside the organization, and visiting other organizations also helps subordinates recognize a need for revitalization. The transformational leader creates a new vision and mobilizes commitment to it by planning or educating others. They build trust through demonstrating personal expertise, self-confidence, and personnel integrity. Finally, the transformational leader must institutionalize the change by replacing old technical, political, cultural, and social networks with new ones.

Effective transformational leaders can motivate subordinates to achieve beyond their original expectations by increasing their awareness of the importance of designated outcomes and ways of attaining them; by getting workers to go beyond their self-interest to that of the team, the department, the university system, and the larger society; and by changing or expanding the individual's needs. Subordinates report they work harder for such leaders. Furthermore, such leaders are judged higher in leadership potential by their subordinates as compared to the more common transactional leader.

One should be cognizant, however, of the negative side of charismatic leadership, which may exist if the leader overemphasizes devotion to themself, makes personal needs paramount, or uses highly effective communication skills to mislead or manipulate others. Such leaders may be so driven to achieve a vision that they ignore the costly implications of their goals.

The administrative leader who overexpands their jurisdiction in an effort to form an "empire of support," only to have the massive system turn into a bureaucratic nightmare, is an example of transformational leadership gone sour. Nevertheless, recent research has verified the overall effectiveness of the transformational leadership style when performed authentically to help the organization succeed.

MISSION-CENTRIC LEADERSHIP

A newer model of leadership known as mission-centric leadership describes a collaborative approach to institutional mission development. This practice is key to its success and adoption by stakeholders. The intentionality of the mission sets the stage for the success that is expected to come as a result of acting on it.

When a leader espouses the words driving the work of the organization, they are harnessing a mission-centric leadership style. While this style is also known in different fields as mission-driven leadership, the tenets remain the same: utilizing the organization's collective purpose and vision to inform governance, leadership, strategy, culture, community impact, programming, and future direction.

It has been said that better outcomes are directly linked to fulfilling the promises of the mission statement. Leaders with this focus are not task oriented. This difference implores mission-centric leaders to be moral agents of change rather than purveyors of simple task mastery.

In a school setting, this leadership style might influence practices where the organization's mission and vision statements are visible throughout the facilities, meeting agendas begin with a centering exercise about mission-related mindedness, and/or the institutional mission statement is used as a way to determine the most appropriate resolution to a difficult decision. Importantly, mission-centric leadership is often linked to mission-driven learning initiatives, pedagogical practice, and people-centered leadership mindedness (Dufresne et al., 2015).

INSTRUCTIONAL LEADERSHIP MODEL

Instructional leadership is commonly referenced in K-12 settings. However, it has implications for practice in higher education environments as well. This leadership style is defined by the National Association of Elementary School Principals (2008) as a practice guiding the way learning communities are developed and led. Within this praxis, staff members regularly meet to discuss their work, collaborate in problem solving, reflect on their profession, and hold themselves accountable for student learning.

Given this definition, one might ask, What is a higher education leader's responsibility as an instructional leader? Murphy (1988) outlines four major dimensions of instructional leadership and the responsibilities of leaders who serve under this model: (1) mission, vision, and goal development; (2) curriculum and instruction management; (3) academic learning climate monitoring and promotion; and (4) work environment stability and growth. While these dimensions can be executed linearly, they are often approached in tandem or in a non-sequential order.

In higher education settings, instructional leaders might work with individual faculty members to assist in pedagogical improvement, modeling instructional strategies, peer observation, co-teaching, co-planning lessons and units, and giving critical feedback for success. Within this practice, coaching is known to be an important component of instructional leadership.

The current widespread practice of professional learning communities (PLCs) in K-12 education is said to have derived from instructional leadership models. And while this practice is not widely used in higher education, the success of PLCs in K-12 would suggest similar wins in post-secondary application.

AN EFFECTIVE LEADERSHIP FORMULA

For concrete or sequential thinkers, it is often clearer and more understandable if a complex theory such as situational leadership theory can be put in mathematical terms. The following is my attempt to do so:

$$\text{Effective Leadership Behavior} = \text{(is a function of)}$$
$$\underline{St + Hr + Pl + Sy}\ (\text{Moral})\ \text{Readiness,}$$

where *St* represents structural frame behavior, *Hr* characterizes human resource behavior, *Pl* is political frame behavior, *Sy* denotes symbolic frame behavior, *Moral* represents moral frame behavior, and *Readiness* signifies the maturity (the ability and willingness to perform the task) level of the follower(s).

Thus, one would articulate this formula in the following manner: effective leadership behavior is the result of or the function of the appropriate application of one or some combination of structural, human resource, political, and symbolic frame behavior, depending on the readiness level of the followers, with the moral frame being a constant.

IMPLICATIONS FOR EDUCATION

The implications of leadership theory for educational administrators are rather clear. The successful administrator needs to have a sound grasp of leadership theory and the skills to implement it (Palestini, 2013). The principles of situational and transformational leadership theory are guides to effective administrative behavior. The leadership behavior applied to an inexperienced faculty member may be significantly different than that applied to a more experienced and tested one. Task behavior or structural frame behavior may be appropriate in dealing with a new staff member, while relationship behavior or human resource frame behavior may be more appropriate when dealing with a seasoned employee.

The four frames of leadership discussed by Bolman and Deal may be particularly helpful to university and college administrators. Consideration of the structural, human relations, political, and symbolic implications of leadership behavior can keep an administrator attuned to the various dimensions affecting appropriate leadership behavior.

Political frame considerations may be particularly helpful in understanding the complexity of relationships and other power issues that exist between administrators and groups such as collective bargaining entities and school boards. Asking oneself the questions posed earlier under the political frame can be an effective guide to the appropriate leadership behavior in dealing with these groups.

The Hersey/Blanchard model, however, may be particularly enlightening in recognizing the importance of employee readiness level and the need to adapt one's leadership style to the readiness level of the follower.

Recently, a plethora of research studies have been conducted on leadership and leadership styles. The overwhelming evidence indicates there is no singular leadership style that is universally appropriate in all situations. Rather, leadership style should be adapted to the situation, so at various times task behavior or relationship behavior might be appropriate. At other times and in other situations, various degrees of both task and relationship behavior should prevail for effectiveness.

EMERGENCE OF TRANSFORMATIONAL LEADERSHIP THEORY

The emergence of transformational leadership theory has seen leadership theory come full circle. Transformational leadership theory combines aspects of the early trait theory perspective with the more current situational or contingency models. The personal charisma of the leader, along with their ability to formulate an educational vision and to communicate it to others, determines the transformational leader's effectiveness.

Since the effective leader is expected to adapt their leadership style to an ever-changing environment, administrative decision-making becomes an even more complex and challenging task. However, a thorough knowledge of leadership theory can help bring clarity and appropriate action to the apparent chaos the administrator faces on an almost daily basis.

IMPLICATIONS FOR PRACTICE: APPLICABLE LEADERSHIP THEORIES AND CONCEPTUAL MODELS CASE STUDY

Bar Harbour University (BHU) is a fifty-year-old private liberal arts college located off the coast of Maine. BHU employs 100 faculty (both tenured and adjunct) and an additional 250 employees (administrators, staff, and contract labor). The president of BHU is Dr. Barelli, who came to the university from a smaller college with strong credentials as a leader in advanced performing and fine arts studies. In the university's relatively short history, there have been only two previous institutional leaders. Under previous presidencies, the organizational structure at BHU was very traditional, and it was supported by a very rich organizational culture.

As the new president, Dr. Barelli sincerely wants to transform BHU. She wants to prove that new technologies and advanced management techniques can make BHU one of the best liberal art schools in the country. To that end, Dr. Barelli creates a vision statement that is displayed throughout the institution. The two-page statement, which has a strong democratic tone, describes the overall purposes, directions, and values of the school.

During the first three years of Dr. Barelli's tenure as president, several major reorganizations took place at the university. These were designed by Dr. Barelli and a select few of her senior executive staff. The intention of each reorganization was to implement advanced organizational structures to bolster the declared BHU vision.

Yet the major outcome of each of the changes was to dilute the leadership and create a feeling of instability among the faculty, administration, and staff. Most changes were made from the top down, from those outside executive leadership positions. Some of the changes gave employees more control in circumstances where they needed less, whereas other changes limited employee input in contexts where employees should have been given more input.

There are some situations in which individual staff report to three different supervisors, and other situations in which department heads have far too many direct reports to oversee. Rather than feeling comfortable in their various roles at BHU, employees begin to feel uncertain about their responsibilities and how they contribute to the stated goals of the institution. The overall effect of the reorganizations is a precipitous drop in employee morale, a lack of quality teaching, and fewer administrative proficiencies.

In the midst of all the changes, the vision that Dr. Barelli had for the school is lost. The instability employees feel makes it difficult for them to support the institution's vision. People at BHU complain that although mission statements are displayed throughout the university campus, no one has a clear idea of the direction the school is going in.

To the employees at BHU, Dr. Barelli is an enigma. BHU had been a great school that produced amazing graduates. Dr. Barelli claims to be democratic in her style of leadership, but she is arbitrary in how she treats faculty and staff. For some she displays a nondirective style, while she is very controlling toward others. She wants to be seen as a hands-on leader, but she often delegates operational control of the university to others while she focuses on external relations and board of trustee matters.

At times Dr. Barelli appears to be insensitive to employees' concerns. Although she wants BHU to be an environment in which everyone feels empowered, she often fails to listen closely to what faculty and staff are saying. She seldom engages in open, two-way communication.

BHU has a long, rich history with many unique stories, but the faculty, administration, and staff feel Dr. Barelli either misunderstands or does not care about their institution's history.

Four years after arriving at BHU, Dr. Barelli steps down as president after her vice president of financial operations runs the university into debt, causing a cash flow crisis. Her dream of building BHU into a world-renowned institution is never realized.

DIAGNOSTIC DEBRIEF

Here are some questions that may be helpful in assessing the effectiveness of the leadership in an institution:

- What aspects of Dr. Barelli's approach created a problematic setting at BHU?
- How might Dr. Barelli have created a more inclusive and trusting organizational culture for BHU?
- Suppose you were an executive coach for Dr. Barelli, what would you tell her to do differently if she had the chance to return as president of BHU?
- In general, what necessary behaviors, required for effective leadership, must administrators display?
- How do institutional leaders encourage the appropriate amount of participation in decision-making?
- How must leaders adapt their leadership behavior to the readiness levels of their followers?
- What attributes must be embraced for effective transformation, a process seeking continuous improvement?
- What benefits might come from leaders operating in all five frames of organizational leadership?

Chapter 4

Mindset for Motivational Change

> Exceptional people convert life's setbacks into future successes.... With the right mindset and the right teaching, people are capable of a lot more than we think.
>
> —*Carol Dweck*

Student achievement, in both K-12 and in higher education, continues to fuel discourse among scholars, administration, policymakers, and educational leaders. But how should student achievement be measured?

In K-12 settings, scholars support rankings, ratings, and percentages of student proficiency based on calculations across standardized measures, while those in opposition argue for a holistic evaluation of student growth. In higher education, colleges and universities continue to discuss the efficacy of SAT/ACT scores as factors for college admission. Challengers to the use of standardized test scores for enrollment decision-making continue to place higher value on high school GPA and college essays as criteria for admission. Regardless of the practice, the end result remains the same: a desire to help students achieve success and to measure academic growth.

The aspirations of educators and educational leaders exploring a hope-filled promise toward increased student growth and success support the work of Dweck's model of growth mindset. Her model serves as a backdrop for investigating the differences between fixed and growth mindsets.

GROWTH MINDSET

People feel comfortable with dichotomous choices—that is, they often prefer situations where dualistic options help narrow selections to just two considerations. So, while there may be many alternative choices, there is comfort in a simplistic model of dualistic comparison. Carol Dweck employs this premise in her model for mindset.

Dweck's (2008) mindset model explains that there are two different ways that one can approach difficult challenges. Those who subscribe to fixed-mindedness believe talents are innate gifts, while those who subscribe to a growth mindset believe talents are developed through perseverance, dedication, strategic planning, and collaboration from and with others.

An example of leading with a growth mindset is when a person fails to complete a seemingly insurmountable task but articulates the belief that they will be able to accomplish the task in the future, once they have acquired more skills (Seaton, 2018). In elementary settings, one might hear this in a second-grade math class when a student replies, "I'm no good at subtraction," and the teacher responds, "Not yet." In college, a star athlete fails to successfully complete a high bar jump and is reminded by their coach, "Not yet." This ostensibly simple phrase reestablishes a *can-do* attitude and focus.

Although differences between fixed and growth mindsets may appear nuanced, they matter. Of considerable interest is the role of *effort*. The belief that effort can lead to mastery of a new skill provides opportunity to explore failure as an essential part of the learning process. Explained as temporary setbacks, failure is often expected as an outcome of trying something new, but, more importantly, it is deemed necessary for growth. Combined with attributes for embracing challenges, accepting critical feedback from others, and the inclination to be motivated by and learn from the success of others, leaders with a growth mindset are poised for success.

PRAISE AND REPRIMAND

Blanchard and Johnson suggest that managers utilize praise and reprimand as motivational devices in an organization. This flows from their first "secret" of effective management: goal setting. Goal-setting theory suggests that setting difficult but attainable goals that are mutually agreed upon can be a powerful motivator (Blanchard & Johnson, 1982; Goncalves, 2012).

Setting goals like higher graduation rates or lower employee dissatisfaction helps focus behavior and motivate individuals to achieve the desired end. However, in order for goal setting to be an effective motivator, the individual involved needs feedback on whether movement toward attaining the goal is progressing adequately. This is where praise and reprimands come into play. It is important that administrators keep their staff abreast of the adequacy of employee performance. When educational leaders are very specific and clear, both praise and reprimands can be effective sources of motivation.

Reprimand the *behavior* only, not the *person*. Thus, the feedback and the individual's reaction to it are about the specific behavior and not their feelings about themselves as human beings. It is sometimes a good idea to follow or precede a reprimand with praise. Make certain the staff member knows their behavior is not okay, but they (as a person) are okay.

Reinforcement theory applies behaviorist learning theories to motivation and has implications for the effectiveness of praise and reprimands. This theory emphasizes the importance of feedback and rewards in motivating desired behavior through diverse reinforcement techniques, including positive reinforcement, like praise, and negative consequences, like reprimands.

Positive reinforcement involves actively encouraging a desired behavior by repeatedly praising or rewarding desired behaviors or outcomes. This feedback shapes behavior by encouraging the reinforced or rewarded behavior to recur.

If behavior is not precisely what is desired by the administrator, repeated reinforcements resulting in successive approximations to the desired behavior can move the actual behavior closer to the desired behavior. For example, if a provost wants their faculty to provide more interactive classroom instruction, the provost might compliment faculty when a cooperative learning activity is included in classroom instruction, and when other interactive techniques are used, additional praise may be given. Praise and other incentives can be used until the best performance occurs.

Punishment, however, actively eliminates undesirable behaviors by applying an undesirable reinforcer (reprimand) to an undesirable behavior. Although it can be effective in eliminating undesirable behavior, punishment can produce anger and bitterness and can be counterproductive in the long run.

Because of the possible negative aftereffects of punishment, administrators must be careful to reprimand infrequently, and, when doing so, to reprimand the undesirable behavior and not the individual. When possible, a reprimand should be followed or preceded by praising the individual. "Your teaching instruction today was somewhat poorly conceived, but I know you have the ability to do better" is an example of reprimanding the behavior and praising the individual. In goal-setting theory, praising and reprimanding are just two ways to motivate faculty and staff. There are a number of other ways of doing so.

NEEDS THEORIES

Suppose the vice president for enrollment management, a senior executive university leader, makes $200,000 a year, and an admissions counselor only earns $55,000. And suppose the board of trustees decides to base part of annual salary increases on whether the university meets its enrollment goals. Why would the board think this policy might motivate its employees? Early motivation theorists would explain such a situation by saying the board expects the new policy to meet the employees' *needs*—their basic requirements for living and working productively.

How does one identify employees' needs? To do a good job of identifying them, the leader probably would need to spend a great deal of time talking with the employees and observing their behavior both inside and outside of the work environment. Many times, determining employees' needs outside of the work environment is conjecture. In the example given earlier, one might conjecture that such a policy might meet the employees' achievement motive.

In this section, two seminal (and widely popular) needs theories are presented: Maslow's hierarchy of needs theory and William Glasser's control theory. Each of these theories describes a specific set of needs the researchers believe individuals have, and each differs somewhat in the number and kinds of needs identified.

MASLOW'S HIERARCHY OF NEEDS

In 1935, Abraham Maslow developed the first needs theory, and it is still one of the most popular and well-known theories of motivation. Maslow stated that individuals have five needs, arranged in a hierarchy from the most basic to the most advanced, as shown in **Figure 4.1**: physiological, safety and security, belongingness and love, esteem, and self-actualization (Maslow, 1987).

Physiological needs are the most basic needs an individual has. These include, at a minimum, a person's requirement for food, water, shelter, and the ability to care for their family. Providing employees with a living wage and medical and dental coverage would help satisfy this need.

Safety needs include a person's desire for security or protection. This translates most directly into concerns for short-term and long-term job security, as well as physical safety at work.

Sense of belonging and the need for love focus on the social aspects of work and nonworking situations. Virtually all individuals desire affectionate relationships or regular interaction with others, which can become a key facet of job design.

Esteem needs relate to a person's desire to master their work, demonstrate competence, build a reputation as an outstanding performer, hold a position of prestige, receive public recognition, and feel self-confident.

Self-actualization needs reflect an individual's desire to grow and develop to their fullest potential. An individual often wants the opportunity to be creative on the job or desires autonomy, responsibility, and challenge.

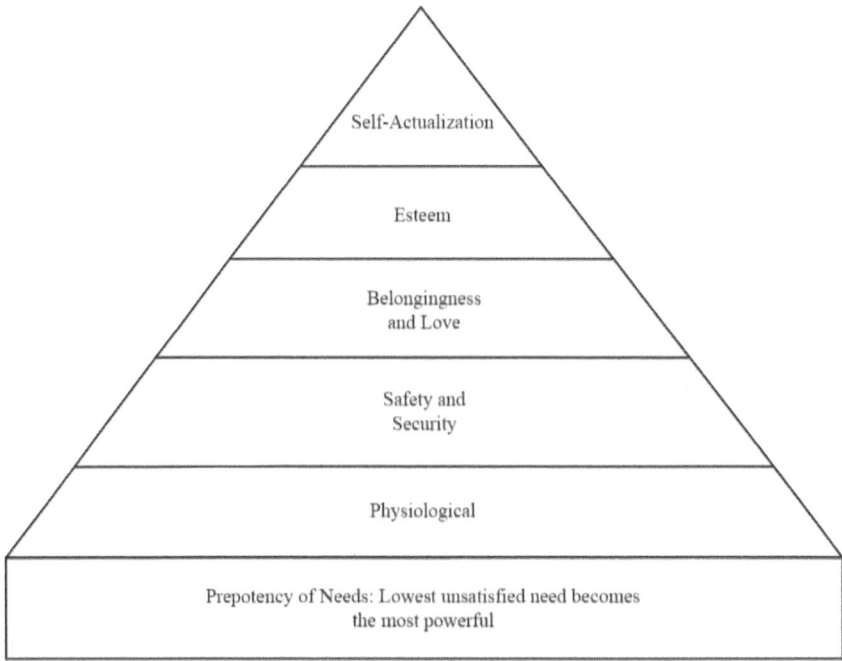

Figure 4.1. Maslow's Hierarchy of Needs

According to needs theory, organizations must meet unsatisfied needs in order to motivate their employees. In Maslow's scheme, the lowest unsatisfied need, starting with the basic physiological needs and continuing through safety, belonging and love, esteem, and self-actualization, becomes the prepotent or most powerful and significant need.

Although the order may vary in certain special circumstances, generally the prepotent need motivates an individual to act to fulfill it; satisfied needs do not motivate. If, for example, a person lacks sufficient food and clothing, they will act to satisfy those basic physiological needs; hence, this person would most likely work to receive pay or other benefits to satisfy those needs. However, a person whose physiological, safety, and belongingness needs are satisfied will be motivated to satisfy needs at the next level, the esteem needs. For this person, pay will not motivate performance unless it increases esteem through a promotion or other changes in job title or status.

Consider again the example of the college that attached salary increases to whether the college reached its recruitment goals. Using Maslow's theory to diagnose the likely effectiveness of the new policy, three questions can be asked: (1) Which needs have already been satisfied? (2) Which unsatisfied need is lowest in the hierarchy? (3) Can those needs be satisfied with the new policy? If, for example, the physiological and safety needs have been satisfied, then the social needs become prepotent; if the new policy can satisfy those needs, which is unlikely, then, according to Maslow's theory, it would be motivating. In this example, then, it is likely that the new policy would satisfy the teachers' and administrators' achievement or self-esteem needs.

CONTROL THEORY

William Glasser (1984) suggests individuals strive to gain control over their emotions and behavior so they will have healthier and more productive lives. His control theory posits individuals are born with five basic human needs: survival, love, power, fun, and freedom. These needs must be satisfied in order for individuals to be productive in their professional and private lives. According to Glasser, people need to control their own behavior so as to make the most need-satisfying choices possible.

The survival need is the innate desire of individuals to be safe and secure. Love and belonging refer to the need for affiliation and affirmation. Power is the need to obtain knowledge and expertise. To Glasser (1984), knowledge is power. The inalienable right to the pursuit of happiness is an effort to fulfill the need for fun. And the opportunity to make free choices is what Glasser believes satisfies the need for freedom.

Effective managers will see that these five needs are satisfied if their employees are expected to be productive. Coercion and competition are counterproductive. Quality performance, therefore, cannot be achieved in an adversarial setting. Workers will perform if coerced, but they will not perform in a quality manner. Competition enables one person to succeed while others fail. Cooperation, however, allows for many winners.

Although Glasser's (1984) control theory has not been verified by empirical research, it has been demonstrated to be successful in a number of school system settings, including the Johnson City, New York, school district, where standardized achievement test scores increased dramatically when Glasser's techniques were used. The faculty was also judged to be more productive when programs that satisfied the five basic needs were implemented.

UTILIZATION OF NEEDS THEORIES

Despite some caveats, needs theory can be utilized effectively in educational settings. When an educational leader is developing or refining program and organizational goals, they should analyze each component with the various needs in mind to be certain that some aspect of the activity or policy addresses one or more of the common needs. For example, if a student organization adviser is preparing a program, they should go through Glasser's (1984) or another theorist's needs theory to see if the program addresses the learner's needs for survival, love, power, fun, and freedom.

In the same way, if an administrator is implementing a total quality management initiative or some other organizational development program at their institution, the leader should incorporate facets that would satisfy each of the faculty's and staff's needs in some significant way.

GOAL-SETTING THEORY

Although extensive research has been conducted on the goal-setting process and its relationship to performance, this section highlights only a sample of the findings. Goals, which any member of an organization can set, describe a desired future state, such as lower absenteeism, higher standardized test scores, higher teacher and staff satisfaction, or specified performance levels. Once established, they can focus behavior and motivate individuals to achieve the desired end state (Vance & Colella, 1990).

Goals can vary in at least three ways: specificity, difficulty, and acceptance. The specificity or clarity of goals refers to the extent to which their accomplishment is observable and measurable. "Reducing college drop-out rates by 5 percent" is a highly specific goal for a university; "all students achieving" is a much less specific goal. Goal difficulty, or the level of performance desired, can also vary significantly. An institutional leader might set a goal to recruit 2 percent more students from abroad or to offer a 50 percent discounted tuition rate to all incoming students; the first goal might be relatively easy to accomplish, the second extremely difficult.

Although goal-setting research originally called for setting moderately difficult goals, current empirical studies indicate that a linear relationship exists between goal difficulty and performance. Empirical studies that combined the two characteristics of goal specificity and difficulty showed that people performed better when they set specific, difficult goals than when they set vague, nonquantitative ones. Individuals' acceptance of stated goals, or their commitment to accomplishing the goals, may vary. In general, a subordinate is less likely to accept a goal as their own and try to accomplish it if a manager assigns the goal rather than jointly sets it with the subordinate.

REDESIGN OF WORK

Work redesign modifies specific jobs to increase both the quality of the employees' work experience and their performance. A job, as a central concern in work design, is defined simply as a set of tasks grouped together under one job title; for example, the roles of administrator, coach, faculty member, president, dean, and custodian are designed to be performed by a single individual. Moreover, jobs are bureaucratic, they are part of the organization, they exist independently of job incumbents, and they are relatively static.

Jobs do change, but not on a day-to-day basis. As a strategy for motivation and change, then, work redesign programs alter the content and process of jobs to match the work motivation of individuals. That is, work redesign efforts modify the school organization to enhance educator and student motivation. The approach to work redesign that will be considered here is succession planning.

SUCCESSION PLANNING

As a redesign of educational work, succession planning programs help ensure longevity of process and continuity of efficient workflow when someone decides to leave (whether for the short term, long term, or permanently). Such programs seek to ensure leadership sustainability in the wake of staffing changes.

There are several reasons generally offered as rationale for succession planning. The first is based on the notion that very few people will remain in their current position or place of employment more than three to five years. Some scholars report more aggressive workplace migration or transience, with the average employee only staying twelve to eighteen months at one particular place of employment.

Still, it is speculated that people in the education field tend to move around less than those in other disciplines or fields of work. Succession planning allows the workforce to be prepared for expected or even unexpected employee departures, affording continuity of critical work functions.

The second reason for succession planning is its ability to allow for cross-functional training. In this way, shared tasks and project-based learning can flourish. When employees enhance their learned skills and competency, they are more poised to assume a leadership role in times of uncertainty. This can sometimes lead to permanent promotion when a designated interim successor assumes ownership for a new functional responsibility and excels.

Lastly, succession planning is professional development. For decades, noted scholars have reported the benefits of professional development opportunities for an organization's workforce. Organization-provided professional development not only keeps employees engaged in the learning process but also demonstrates a level of care on behalf of the organization to its team members.

There are those who might show opposition to succession planning as its practice might scare upper management as though their job is always being chased by a subordinate for replacement. To this we provide the following adage: A university president asks their human resources leader, "What happens if we invest in developing our people and then they leave us?" To which the HR leader replies, "What happens if we don't and they stay?"

Succession planning programs redesign jobs to provide individuals with prospects for promotion, to ensure workplace continuity, and to provide professional development opportunities. In essence, the goal of succession planning is to enrich work and enlarge workforce capacity. Succession planning, as a job enrichment model, generally includes opportunities for growth in learning skills and developing competencies. It can also provide mentorship for those learning a new skill.

IMPLICATIONS FOR PRACTICE: MINDSET FOR MOTIVATIONAL CHANGE CASE STUDY

A transgender woman student, Ariel, fully participates in the formal sorority recruitment process. While she feels all the groups are inclusive and welcome her participation, one chapter really shows interest in her joining, and there appears to be strong alignment between the organization, their membership, and Ariel's values.

The current membership is very diverse, with members having varied racial, ethnic, and religious identities. However, Ariel would be their first transgender woman. Ariel is used to being the first gender-diverse person in spaces. Still, she has to overcome her anxiety and reluctance before she feels comfortable accepting the invitation to join.

While she feels included by the undergraduate membership of the sorority, Ariel can't help feeling *watched* by a few alumnae she spoke with at recruitment events. This feeling of unease gives her pause, but ultimately she reasons she will mostly be engaging with the current undergraduate members and will likely have limited interactions with sorority alumnae.

In the two weeks leading up to new member initiation, Ariel feels safe and welcomed by her sorority sisters and her new member class. However, two days before new member initiation is scheduled to take place, a representative from the sorority's national headquarters contacts the undergraduate chapter president to inform them that organizational bylaws prohibit men from becoming members of the sorority. The undergraduate chapter president attempts to explain that Ariel identifies as a woman, not as a man, but the national representative is not interested in debating this issue.

DIAGNOSTIC DEBRIEF

Here are some questions that might be used to assess an institution's motivational processes:

- Do the rewards of membership provided satisfy the variety of individual needs?
- Is a full range of motivational tools being used by the chapter president?
- Are rewards both internal and external?
- Are rewards applied equitably and consistently?
- Is reinforcement theory (praising and reprimanding) being employed effectively?
- Do individuals set goals as a source of motivation (goal-setting theory)?
- Are the rewards and incentives effective in motivating desired behaviors?

Chapter 5

Effective Decision-Making

> Your choices and decisions are a reflection of how well you've set and followed your priorities.
>
> —*Elizabeth George*

Suppose Dr. Melissa Garza was appointed to the position of university president for Leon Valley University (LVU) with the express purpose of rightsizing the institution in light of its declining undergraduate enrollment. Having been successful in a similar situation at another college, how should Dr. Garza proceed?

There are two aspects Dr. Garza must immediately bring to the forefront in the decision-making process—namely, the decision's *quality* and its *acceptance*. A high-quality decision brings about the desired result while meeting relevant criteria and constraints. What would constitute a high-quality decision in the situation at LVU? Certainly, a decision that reduces costs while maintaining educational quality would be considered a high-quality one. Also, a decision that meets the needs of those affected by the decision—including students, faculty, staff, administrators, and alumni—would qualify; so too would a decision that meets the financial, human, time, and other constraints of the situation.

The level of the decision maker's technical or task skills, interpersonal or leadership skills, and decision-making skills can affect the quality of the decision. Technical or task skills refer to the individual's knowledge of the particular area in which the decision is being made. In the decision Dr. Garza must make about rightsizing, task skills refer to a knowledge of labor costs, projected revenues, educational product information, school system overhead costs, and past experience.

Interpersonal or leadership skills relate to the way individuals lead, communicate with, motivate, and influence others. Dr. Garza, for example, must be able to convince the other stakeholders in the organization system to accept the decision for which she is responsible. Dr. Garza and any advisers she involves in the decision-making process must produce a decision that they and the rest of the school system community can accept. Their concluding judgment is one in which they will face reputational risk.

For example, sunsetting (i.e., closing) two academic programs may be a high-quality decision, but collective tenured faculty may oppose this decision so vehemently that the decision may be inoperable. Alternatively, reducing the administrative support staff and increasing class size (by lowering admission criteria) may be a high-quality decision, but parents of incoming students might resist the change because they feel their children risk receiving a lower-quality education. Thus, *acceptance* of the decision by the stakeholders is a characteristic that needs to be considered along with the *quality* of the decision.

VROOM-YETTON DECISION-MAKING MODEL

Administrative and organizational theory literature agrees about the two most important factors to be considered in determining the decision style that will produce the most effective decisions. While Vroom and Yetton's model includes the additional dimensions of shared goals and conflict possibility, the two key elements are the *quality* and the *acceptance* of the decision, as described above (Lührs et al., 2018). **Figure 5.1** summarizes the identification of the decision style that is most appropriate for particular problem types (Vroom & Jago, 1988; Vroom & Yetton, 1973).

The two key elements are *quality*, or the likelihood of one decision to be more rational and right than another, and *acceptance*, or the extent to which acceptance or commitment on the part of stakeholders is crucial to the effective implementation of the decision. For instance, if a new law is passed regarding the education of students with disabilities and the administrator has to decide how to communicate this to the educational community, the quality of the decision would be more important than its acceptance. Therefore, the appropriate decision style is *command*. However, if acceptance is more important than quality, as in the development of a new faculty evaluation instrument, the proper decision style would be *consensus*. If both the quality and acceptance are of equal importance—for example, when deciding whether to adopt a whole language approach to reading instruction—*consultation* or group decision-making would be the appropriate style. Finally, if neither the quality nor the acceptance is important, like deciding what color to paint the inside of the school closets, *convenience* would be the applicable style.

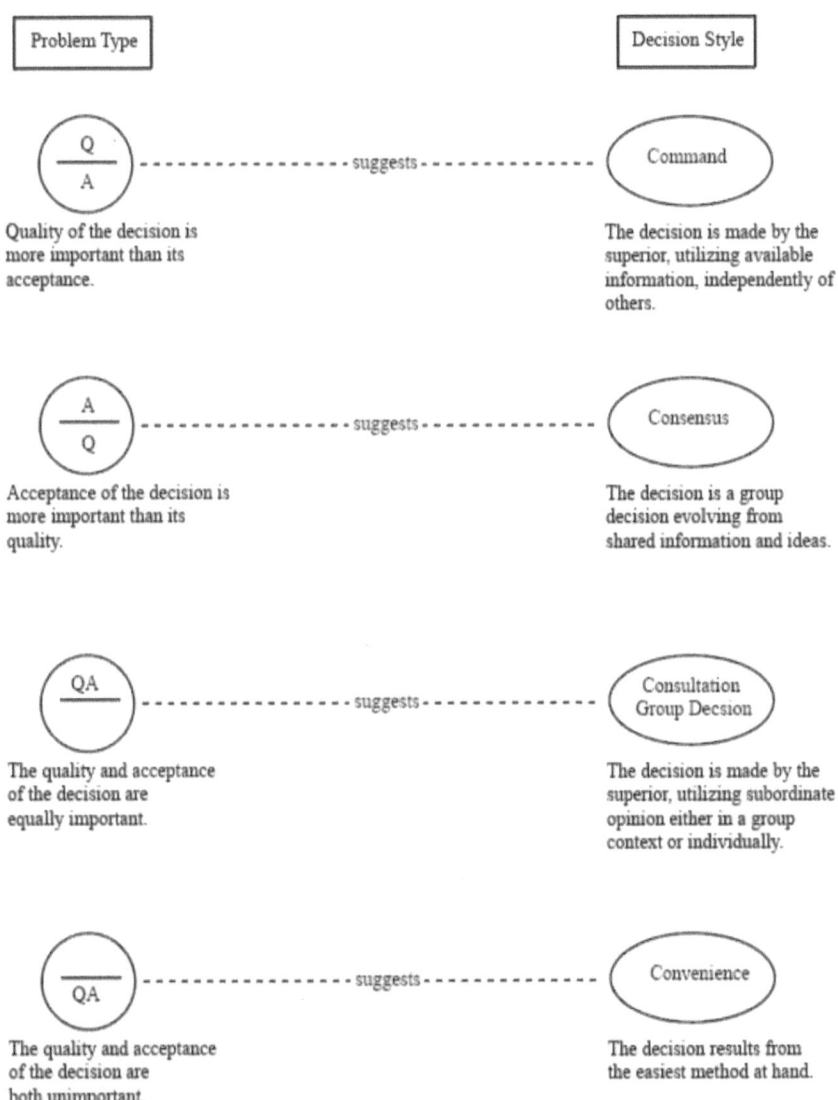

Figure 5.1. The Dimensions of Effective Decisions

ETHICAL DECISION-MAKING

One can also assess how well a decision meets the criterion of ethical fairness and justice in addition to evaluating it in terms of its quality and acceptance. Consider, for example, a disastrous decrease in the college graduation rate at a certain institution. Top administrators are faced with the decision of whether to risk public scrutiny and the possible transfer of significant numbers of students or to ignore the situation.

Administrators and staff can assess whether the decisions they make are ethical by applying personal moral codes or society's codes of values, they can apply philosophical views of ethical behavior, or they can assess the potential harmful consequences of behaviors to certain constituencies (Jones, 1991). A valuable tool in the ethical decision-making process could be the application of a mission-centered leadership approach as discussed in chapter 3 (Rest, 1986).

GROUP DECISION-MAKING

Individuals or groups can apply the decision-making processes described thus far, but group decision-making brings different resources to the task or situation than does individual decision-making. When a group makes a decision, a synergy occurs that often causes the group decision to be better than the sum of the individual decisions.

The involvement of more than one individual brings additional knowledge and skills to the decision, and it tends to result in higher-quality decisions. However, the same caveat holds for decision-making as has been reiterated throughout this book. That is, decision-making is situational, and the idiosyncrasies of the moment dictate the decision-making approach to be taken. For example, if a building is on fire, participative decision-making is obviously not appropriate.

GROUP DIVERSITY AND INCLUSIVE PRACTICE

As the group becomes more diverse in terms of attitude, behavior, and culture, the advantages of diversity increase. Diversity provides the greatest asset for teams with difficult, discretionary tasks requiring innovation.

A team's diversity can also be helpful when working on simple tasks involving repetitive and routine procedures. Thus, when establishing a committee or task force to address a complex problem, be certain that its membership reflects the various stakeholders of the institution's community. Take particular interest in categories of diversity beyond race, religion, position title, or geographic location. Other categories for consideration might include, but are not limited to, gender, age, education level, experience level, intellectual ability, and physical ability.

Inclusive practice is a by-product of group diversity. As a teaching approach, it seeks to recognize differences between students. It then harnesses group diversity to ensure that all participants in the classroom environment can access educational content with full participation in the learning process. Inclusive practice celebrates differences in all people, and in doing so influences a decision-making praxis in which learning objectives, instruction, and assessments accommodate individuals' diverse needs.

Creating a safe, respectful, trusting, and inclusive group dynamic is a team effort. Despite reflected differences in race, culture, age, religion, sexual orientation, socioeconomic background, and other social identities and life experiences, the goal of inclusiveness, in a diverse community, encourages and appreciates expressions of different ideas, opinions, and beliefs, so conversations and interactions that could potentially be divisive turn instead into opportunities for intellectual and personal enrichment.

A dedication to inclusiveness requires respecting what others say and their right to say it, and the thoughtful consideration of others' communication. Both speaking up and listening are valuable tools for furthering thoughtful, enlightening dialogue. Respecting one another's individual differences is critical in transforming a collection of diverse individuals into an inclusive, collaborative, and excellent learning community.

TIME REQUIRED

Individual decision-making generally takes less time than group decision-making. The exchange of information among many individuals, as well as the effort spent on obtaining consensus, is time-consuming. Sometimes, to reach a decision more quickly or to reach a decision all group members will accept, groups "satisfice" rather than optimize. That is, they tend to make decisions that are expedient (Bailey et al., 2018; Simon, 1960).

RISKINESS OF DECISIONS

A plethora of scholarly work suggests groups tend to make riskier decisions. The guiding thought supporting this notion is that no single person shoulders the consequences of the decision made by a group. That is, individuals may feel less accountable and will accept more risk or extreme solutions when working within a group setting. When a problem occurs, people do not forge a complaint against an entire committee; they complain to a single person in leadership. This phenomenon supports riskier decisions being made in group decision-making proceedings.

GROUPTHINK

Irving Janis first identified *groupthink* as a factor influencing the misguided 1961 Bay of Pigs invasion. The symptoms of groupthink arise when members of decision-making groups try to avoid being too critical in their judgment of other group members' ideas and focus too heavily on developing concurrence. It occurs most frequently in highly cohesive groups, particularly in stressful situations.

Group members experiencing groupthink may feel invulnerable to criticism and hence believe that any action they take or decision they make will be positively received. They may also ignore external criticism, choosing instead to rationalize their actions or decisions as optimum. Some group members may also pressure other group members to agree with the group's decision; deviant opinions are either ignored or not tolerated; members can neither question views offered nor offer disconfirming information. All of these aspects were present in the Bay of Pigs decision (Gordon, 1993).

The Bay of Pigs decision can be contrasted with John F. Kennedy's Cuban missile crisis decision made a few years later. In this case, Kennedy learned from the Bay of Pigs mistake and did not allow groupthink to influence the decision-making process, thus yielding dramatically different results.

CHOOSING GROUP DECISION-MAKING

Conventional wisdom concedes to employ group decision-making unless the *acceptance* of the decision is irrelevant. Group decision-making is superior when a task or problem requires a variety of expertise, when problems have multiple parts that can be addressed by a division of labor, and when problems require estimates. Individual decision-making results in more efficiency if policy dictates the correct solution.

Problems requiring the completion of a series of complex stages tend to be solved more effectively through an individual decision-making process, so long as the individual receives input from many sources, as this practice allows better coordination throughout the phases of solving the problem. In Leon Valley University, for example, the main decision Dr. Garza and her colleagues must make is how to reduce costs without reducing quality. This type of problem requires diverse knowledge and skills, creativity, and completion of a series of complex stages, calling most likely for a combination of individual and group decision-making.

Importantly, group decision-making more often leads to acceptance than does decision-making by individuals. In addition, since individuals involved in deciding generally become committed to the outcome, use of group consensus expedites acceptance of the decision by the group, thereby increasing individual and group commitment to the decision. Acceptance of the decision about rightsizing at LVU may affect its implementation in the short run, and since employees cannot easily be replaced, may also affect it in the long run. Therefore, the acceptance is as important as the quality of the decision.

Group decision-making generally leads to higher-quality solutions unless an individual's expertise in the decision areas is identified in the beginning. At LVU, Dr. Garza has had successful experience in rightsizing; therefore, she has less need for group input to make a high-quality decision. However, she needs the input because the acceptance of the decision is so important.

The amount of time available will determine whether group problem solving is feasible because group decision-making takes much more time than individual decision-making. LVU must resolve its problem in a timely manner or risk both internal and external scrutiny; therefore, the amount of group participation may be somewhat limited.

WAYS TO IMPROVE DECISION-MAKING

How can decision makers overcome barriers, reduce biases, and make more effective decisions? Here, three techniques are offered as solutions to improve decision-making: brainstorming, the nominal group technique, and the Delphi technique.

Brainstorming

When creativity is needed, groups or individuals use *brainstorming* to generate many alternatives for consideration in decision-making. In brainstorming, they list as many alternatives as possible without simultaneously evaluating the feasibility of any alternative. For example, Dr. Garza might charge a task force with listing all the ways of reducing costs at LVU.

The absence of evaluation encourages group members to generate rather than defend ideas. Then, after ideas have been generated, they are evaluated, and decisions are made. Although brainstorming can result in many shallow and useless ideas, it can also motivate members to offer new ideas. It works best when individuals have a common view of what constitutes a good idea, but it is harder to use when specialized knowledge or complex implementation is required (Adams, 1986).

Nominal Group Technique

As a structured group meeting, the *nominal group technique* helps resolve differences in group opinion by having individuals generate and then rank order a series of ideas in the problem exploration, alternative generation, or choice-making stages of the process (Michaelson et al., 1989). A group of individuals is presented with a stated problem. Each person individually offers alternative solutions in writing. The group then shares the solutions and lists them on a dry-erase board, large piece of paper, or shared electronic form as in brainstorming. The group discusses and clarifies the ideas. They then rank and vote for their preferred ideas. If the group has not reached an agreement, they repeat the ranking and voting procedure until the group reaches some consensus.

Nominal group technique encourages innovation, limits conflict, emphasizes equal participation by all members, helps generate consensus, and incorporates the preferences of individuals in decision-making choices. However, unless the administrator is trained in the use of this technique and the ones that follow, it would be more prudent to employ an organizational consultant who is trained and has experience in these techniques to act as a facilitator in the process. **Figure 5.2** illustrates the steps in nominal group technique.

Delphi Technique

Four stages are used to structure group communication through the Delphi technique structure. When dealing with a complex problem, Delphi's four phases are (1) exploration of the subject by individuals, (2) reaching understanding of the group's view of the issues, (3) sharing and evaluating any reasons for differences, and (4) final evaluation of all information.

In the conventional Delphi, a small group designs a questionnaire, which is completed by a larger respondent group. The results are then tabulated and used in developing a revised questionnaire, which is again completed by the larger group. Thus, the results of the original polling are fed back to the respondent group to use in subsequent responses. This procedure is repeated until the issues are narrowed, responses are focused, or consensus is reached (Flostrand et al., 2020; Rowe & Wright, 1999; Thomas et al., 1989). Delphi can be very helpful in a variety of circumstances, such as the following:

- When the decision makers cannot apply precise analytical techniques to solving the problem but prefer to use subjective judgments on a collective basis, Delphi can provide input from a large number of respondents.

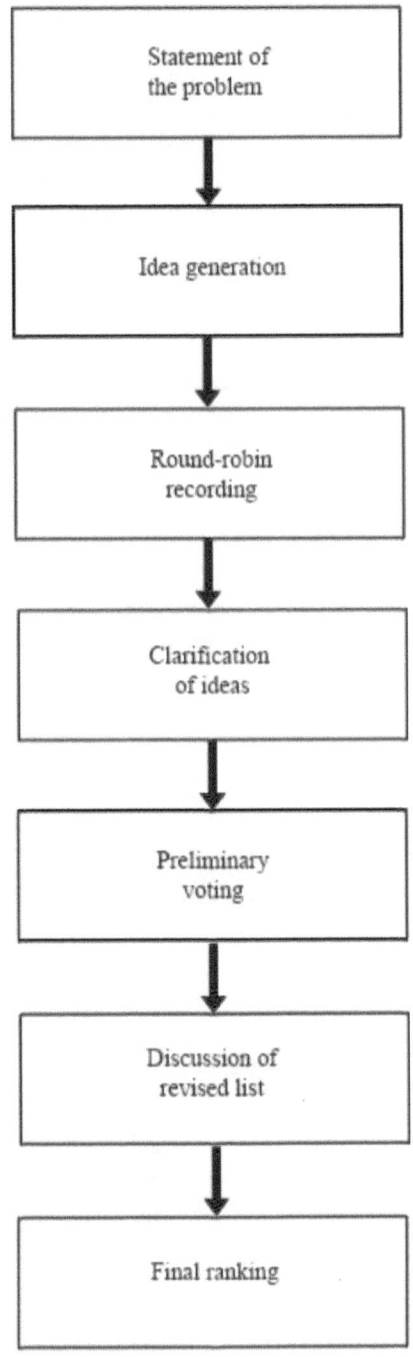

Figure 5.2. Steps in Nominal Grouping

- If the individuals involved have failed to communicate effectively in the past, the Delphi procedures offer a systematic method for ensuring that all opinions are presented.
- Delphi technique does not require face-to-face, place-based interaction and thus succeeds when the group is too large for such a direct exchange.
- When time and cost prevent frequent group meetings or when a pre-meeting communication would be helpful, the Delphi technique offers significant value for decision-making.
- Delphi can also overcome situations where individuals greatly disagree or where the anonymity of views must be maintained to protect group members.
- Finally, the Delphi technique reduces the likelihood of groupthink; it prevents one or more members from dominating positionality through their strength in numbers or the assertiveness of their personality.

Figure 5.3 summarizes the steps of the Delphi technique.

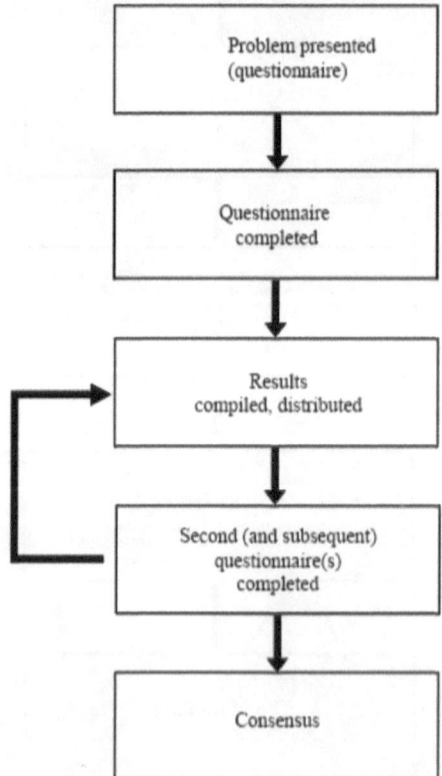

Figure 5.3. Steps in the Delphi Technique

CONCLUSION

Decision-making is a basic and important process in educational institutions. The success experienced by educational administrators depends largely on their mastery and effective implementation of the decision-making process. This chapter describes the nature of the decision being made in rightsizing Leon Valley University.

To make such decisions effectively, individuals must have technical, interpersonal, and decision-making skills. Outlined are basic decision-making processes that help improve the quality of a decision and encourage its acceptance by others. Furthermore, *quality* and *acceptance* are the two most important factors to be considered in rendering a decision. Decision makers must systematically analyze the situation; set objectives; generate, evaluate, and select alternatives; make the decision; and evaluate the decision made.

The systematic, analytical nature of decision-making helps to accentuate the situational nature of effective decision-making. There is no single decision-making style that is more effective in all circumstances and at all times. In response, some techniques can improve decision-making processes. This chapter highlights the benefit and approach of the nominal group technique, brainstorming, and the Delphi technique. Another vital step leading to effective administration includes taking a few minutes each day to determine what decision-making model is best for a given situation.

IMPLICATIONS FOR PRACTICE: EFFECTIVE DECISION-MAKING CASE STUDY

Dr. Stander is the vice president for institutional research and development at a midsized public university that has approximately 1,200 employees (faculty, staff, and administration). As a result of recent reorganization, the university must choose a new director of institutional research (a newly created position).

The research team directly supervised by this position consists of five full-time positions. Selecting the best candidate for the director position is important because Dr. Stander is receiving pressure from the president and board of trustees to improve the institution's overall responsiveness to research demands and performance. This is particularly important in consideration of the looming report due to the Middle States Commission on Higher Education that must be completed by the end of the current academic year.

Dr. Stander has identified three candidates to interview for this position, drawing from eighteen applications in the hiring pool. Each candidate brings a unique set of skills and experiences. The university is having difficulty choosing a finalist because each applicant offers very strong credentials:

- Jean Smith is a longtime employee of the university who started as a part-time graduate assistant in another department under student leadership and activities. After finishing her graduate degree, she has held four different positions at the institution in different offices under both the division of student life and in administrative roles within academic affairs. She is currently the assistant director of institutional research. Performance reviews for Jean's work have repeatedly described her as being creative and insightful. In her tenure, Jean has developed three new assessment models for the institution, which are deployed annually. These models collect information in a more strategic manner from campus departments, helping to centralize data across the campus. Jean is known across the institution as being persistent about her work; when she starts a project, she stays with it until it is finished. It is probably this quality that accounts for the success of each of the three assessment models with which she has been involved.
- A second candidate for the new position is Kelsey Angler. Kelsey previously worked for the institution in enrollment management but left more than five years ago to pursue another opportunity at a different school. Her current title is director of research and data collection at a small private university with approximately 600 employees. Kelsey has a reputation of being very bright. She holds a BA from Harvard and an MS from the University of Pennsylvania, graduating top of her class. People talk about Kelsey as someone who will be vice president at a school someday. Kelsey is very personable. On all her performance reviews, she has received extra-high scores on sociability and human relations. There isn't a supervisor in the university who doesn't have positive memories of working with her when she was an employee there earlier in her career. At her current place of employment, Kelsey co-chairs the committee responsible for ensuring all reports are submitted on time to the Middle States Commission on Higher Education.
- Thomas Sullivan, the third candidate, has never worked for an institution of higher education. He is a self-employed consultant who for the last fifteen years has specialized in strategic planning and executive leadership coaching. Thomas has previously consulted with the university on strategic planning. He is very involved in establishing the institution's vision and is familiar with its mission and goals. The two qualities that stand out above the rest for Thomas are his honesty and integrity. Employees who have worked with Thomas report that they can trust Thomas to provide a fair and consistent assessment. He is highly

respected by many at the institution who have worked with him (many of whom hold leadership roles). Thomas does have experience in institutional research and has worked as a consultant with several schools on their Middle States Commission on Higher Education report processes.

The challenge confronting Dr. Stander is to choose the best person for the newly established director position. She is also struggling to determine how much feedback and group input she should have in this decision. (*Unconscious bias check: Did you imagine Dr. Stander to be a man? If so, ask yourself why.*) Based on the aforementioned pressures from upper leadership and the need to onboard someone quickly to begin working on their annual reporting, Dr. Stander's selection criteria must take into consideration all the responsibilities of this position and office in comparison to the strengths and weaknesses of each candidate.

DIAGNOSTIC DEBRIEF

Here are some questions that may be helpful in assessing the decision-making process in the presented case study and in general at an institution:

- What decision-making process would be helpful to Dr. Stander in selecting a candidate?
- What selection criteria should be used in making this decision?
- Do organizational members make high-quality, accepted, and ethical decisions?
- Do decision makers follow a rational process of decision-making?
- Is the group appropriately involved in decision-making?
- Are techniques such as brainstorming, nominal group, and the Delta techniques being used to facilitate the decision-making process?

Chapter 6

Significance of Communication

> To be a totally alien world in the person of another; we are called upon to use our imaginations to enter into that world, to discover how it looks and feels from the vantage point of the person whose world it is.
>
> —*Maxine Greene*

Communication is often considered the root of all disagreements and misunderstandings (Polevoi, 2012). One of the perennial complaints of employees is a lack of communication between themselves and other segments of the community. Thus, effectively communicating with others is one of the most important skills an educational leader can master.

MODELS AND MODES OF COMMUNICATION

Models used to explain communication processes are plentiful, such as Aristotle's model, Lasswell's model, Shannon-Weaver model, Berlo's S-M-C-R model, Osgood-Schramm model, Westley and Maclean model, Burnlund's transactional model, and Dance's helical model (just to reference a few). These models can be categorized into three types: linear, interactive, and transactional. Linear models seek to illustrate a one-directional communication process, whereas interactive types explore two-way interpersonal communication. The last type, transactional, is used to describe two-way immediate feedback communication processes.

Despite slight variations among the model types, certain components remain consistent. Communication requires a sender, a receiver, and a message. Additional elements in communication processes may include the role of encoding/decoding; feedback; and environmental, cultural, and personal factors. Some components of these models are further described in this chapter.

Similar to the variety of communication model types to consider, there are also different modes of communication available. A mode describes a means of communicating. When researching modal types, it is clear there is much variation in how scholars categorize and cluster types. For example, according to the New London Group, there are five multimodal types of communication: linguistic (written and spoken words), visual (images either moving or still), aural (sound), gestural (movement, expression, body language), and spatial (position, physical arrangement, proximity).

Sharing information between individuals is another consideration to organize modes. Within this type, disseminating data takes place in one of three ways: interpretative (one way), interpersonal (two way), and presentational (one way by addressing a group) communication. Other modal arrangements also exist.

In addition to contrasting models and modes of communication, the delivery method or device employed when communicating can vary (Team Leverage Edu, 2020). There are both verbal and nonverbal methods for consideration. Stories, literature, articles, speeches, songs, radio news, videos, and movies are most prevalent within an interpretative communication mode. By contrast, in an interpersonal mode, social media, text messages, and telephones are often utilized. A presentational mode favors articles, flyers, short stories, reports, presentations, skits, debates, speeches, and so on to communicate.

Based on variabilities among different models, modes, and ways of communicating, it is easy to understand why miscommunication is commonplace. Ensuring communication is concise and clearly understood by an intended receiver means successfully navigating a very complex labyrinth of choices.

COMMUNICATION EFFECTIVENESS

What can individuals do to improve their communication in both formal and informal settings? This section examines three ways of increasing communication effectiveness: creating a supportive communication climate, using an assertive communication style, and using active listening techniques (Drew, 2020).

In communicating with their faculties and staffs, administrators know they must create a trusting and supportive environment. Creating such a climate has the objective of shifting from attribution or blaming to problem solving and staff development (Ärlestig, 2008). Administrators must avoid making employees feel defensive—that is, threatened by the communication (Neubert & Dyck, 2016). An atmosphere where meaningful feedback and open communication can take place may be established in one or any combination of these ways:

1. Using descriptive rather than evaluative speech. Not implying the receiver needs to change. An administrator may describe a supervisee's traits in terms of strengths and areas in need of further development rather than describing them as weaknesses.
2. Employing a clinical approach, which implies a desire to collaborate in exploring a mutual problem rather than trying to control or change the listener. An administrator can ask the supervisee what they hope to achieve in the short term or for the entire academic year rather than setting out a list of preordained goals that the supervisee must merely follow.
3. Using spontaneity and honesty, the administrator may reveal their goals rather than appearing to use "strategy" that involves ambiguity and multiple motivations. For instance, a departmental vice president might share with the department the need for restructuring and possible areas of downsizing rather than doing so surreptitiously.
4. Conveying empathy for their listener's feelings rather than appearing unconcerned or neutral about the listener's welfare. By giving reassurance, the administrator is identifying with the listener's problems rather than denying the legitimacy of the problems. For example, when speaking with a student in a judicial conduct meeting, the hearing officer may indicate sensitivity to the student's position and concerns even though a decision may ultimately go against the student.
5. In conversations between a supervisor and supervisee, the leader indicating and modeling a sense of equality rather than superiority to the listener. This action reinforces a willingness to engage in a shared relationship, not simply one of dominance over another. A college dean may come out from behind their desk and sit next to a colleague to indicate a relationship of equality.
6. Finally, an educational leader communicating they will be flexible regarding their own behavior and ideas rather than taking a dogmatic approach. They express freely when they do not have an answer for a question posed to them and they ask for help when needed. An effective administrator can concede they do not know if their suggestion will work, but they can indicate to the supervisee, "Let's give it a try."

Using complete knowledge of oneself and others is another tested way of improving interpersonal communication. This practice encourages individuals to communicate more openly. The Johari window provides an analytical tool individuals can use to identify information that is available for use in communication. **Figure 6.1** illustrates this model of interpersonal knowledge (Gordon, 1993; Oliver & Duncan, 2019). Note information about an individual is represented along two dimensions: (1) information known and unknown by the self and (2) information known and unknown by others.

Figure 6.1. Johari Window

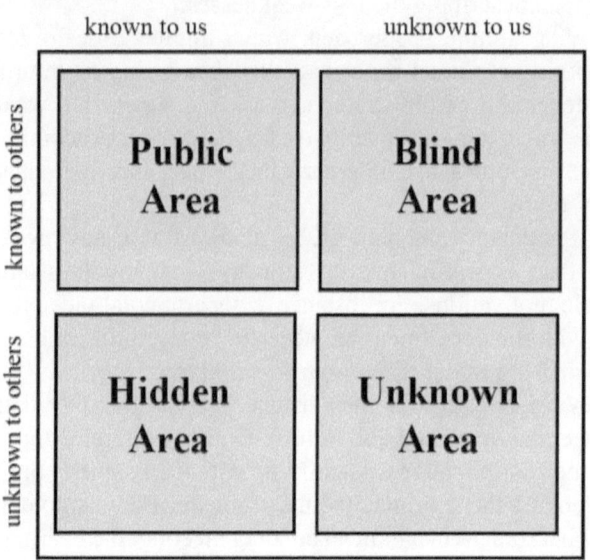

Together these dimensions form a four-category representation of the individual. The open self is information known by the self and known by others. The blind self is information unknown by the self and known by others, such as others' perceptions of your behavior or attitudes. The concealed self is information known by self and unknown by others; secrets kept from others fall into this category (Oliver & Duncan, 2019; Stout & Dasgupta, 2013). Finally, the unconscious self is information that is unknown to the self and unknown to others.

To ensure quality communication, in most cases an individual should communicate from their "open self" to another's open self and limit the amount of information concealed or in the blind spot. Guarded communication may be appropriate, however, if one party has violated trust in the past, if the parties have an adversarial relationship, or if the relationship is transitory (Oliver & Duncan, 2019; Stout & Dasgupta, 2013).

THE ASSERTIVE COMMUNICATION STYLE

Communication can be improved by using an assertive style that is honest, direct, and firm. These stylistic attributes allow a person to express personal needs, opinions, and feelings in an honest and direct way. Assertiveness can allow one to uphold their rights without violating the rights of others. Content and the nonverbal styling of a message can also reflect assertive behavior. The assertive leader, for example, is clear and direct when explaining work to supervisees; doesn't hover; and criticizes fairly, objectively, and constructively.

Consider the situation of a chief financial officer (CFO) whose assistant has missed two important deadlines in the past month. How would the CFO respond assertively? Might the CFO say to their assistant, "I know you missed the last two deadlines. Is there an explanation I should know about? It is important that you meet the next deadlines." An assertive response can include an expression of anger, frustration, or disappointment, but it is structured in an approach that allows for feedback to obtain an explanation for the behavior.

An assertive approach can be further contrasted to unassertive and aggressive styles. Unassertive communication describes behavior where the sender does not stand up for their leadership responsibilities and indicates that their feelings are unimportant; the person may be hesitant, apologetic, or fearful. In the situation of a missed deadline, unassertive behavior might involve the CFO saying nothing to their assistant, hoping the situation will not recur.

Individuals act unassertively because they may mistake assertion for aggression, mistake unassertiveness for politeness or being helpful, refuse to accept their leadership responsibilities, experience anxiety about negative consequences of assertiveness, or lack assertiveness skills (Heasley & Palestini, 2022; Palestini, 2011).

In aggressive communication one expresses their view and rights without respecting the rights of the other person. Aggressive behavior attempts to dominate and control others by sounding accusing or superior. In the situation of the missed deadlines, an aggressive response might be, "You always miss deadlines. You're taking advantage of me and the situation. If you miss another deadline, disciplinary action will be taken."

While such a response may result in the desired behavior in a specific circumstance, its long-term consequences will likely be dysfunctional, resulting in distrust between the individuals involved. Ultimately, such behavior will negatively affect productivity and will especially affect the submission of creative and innovative solutions offered to management by the employee.

EMPLOYING ACTIVE LISTENING TECHNIQUES

Active listening, which requires understanding both the content and the intent of a message, can be facilitated by paraphrasing, perception checking, and behavior description (Arneson, 2015).

The receiver can paraphrase the message conveyed by the sender by stating in their own way what the other person's remarks convey. For example, if the sender states, "I don't like the work I am doing," the receiver might paraphrase it as, "Are you saying you are dissatisfied with being a professor? Or are you dissatisfied with the subject matter you teach? Or do you wish to be teaching online rather than place-based courses?" The way the original message is paraphrased can suggest very different understandings of the original statement. The sender, upon receiving this feedback from the receiver, can then clarify their intentions.

Alternatively, the receiver may provide a perception check—that is, describe what they perceive as the sender's inner state at the time of communication to check understanding of the original message. For example, if the sender states, "I don't like the work I am doing," the receiver might check perception of the statement by asking, "Are you dissatisfied with the tasks you have been given? Are you dissatisfied by the way you are being treated? Or are you dissatisfied with me as a supervisor?" The answers to these three questions will identify different feelings.

Behavior description is the third way of checking communication. Here, the individual reports specific, observable actions of others without making accusations or generalizations about their motives, personality, or characteristics. Similarly, description of feelings, where the individual specifies or identifies feelings by name, analogy, or some other verbal representation, can increase active listening. For example, in the instance cited above, one might say, "You look angry," "You look resentful," or "You seem bitter."

THE VALUE OF FEEDBACK

In addition to a culture of trust and respect, feedback is perhaps the most important aspect of an effective communication process. Feedback refers to an acknowledgment by the receiver that the message has been received; it provides the sender with information about the receiver's understanding of the message being sent.

Often one-way communication occurs between administrators and their colleagues. Because of inherent power differences in their positions, administrators may give large quantities of information and directions to their faculty and staff without providing the opportunity for them to show their understanding or receipt of the information. These managers often experience conflict between their role as an authority figure and a desire to be liked and trusted by their colleagues.

Other administrators rely almost exclusively on the use of written memoranda postings on the faculty/staff bulletin board as a way of communicating. In addition to the inherent lack of feedback involved in this format, the use of a single channel of communication also limits the effectiveness of communication.

The proliferation of the use of email and text messaging has alleviated this problem somewhat by providing a relatively facile feedback mechanism. However, miscommunication and misunderstanding can also be present in electronic modes of communication. Still, encouraging feedback from others shows that leadership is concerned about employees as individuals, in ways that go beyond merely showing they are productive workforce members.

EXTERNAL COMMUNICATION

As was discussed in chapter 1, the open system model of organizational structure highlights the vulnerability and interdependence of organizations and their environments. External environments are important because they affect the internal structures and processes of organizations; hence, one is forced to look both inside and outside the organization to explain behavior within school organizations.

However, the growing necessity to interact with the outside environment places added responsibilities and demands on the school district's communications processes. The need to communicate with parents, government officials, advocacy groups, and the mass media cannot be denied. This necessity, however, is a relatively recent phenomenon and presents difficulties to administrators whose training does not normally include communicating with the public through the mass media.

Although the principles of effective communication still prevail when dealing with the outside community, some nuances need to be stressed. Perhaps the most important aspect of communication that needs to be considered when dealing with the public is the uniformity of the message. The message must be clear and consistent and emanate from a single source. In these cases, the chain of command and channels of communication need to be well defined and structured along the lines of the classical model.

Given considerations in communication, it is imperative the institution speak with one voice. Typically, a marketing and communication department is given the responsibility to communicate with external agencies. This office is positioned as the clearinghouse for such matters. This individual, or office, should review all external communication for clarity and accuracy, and institutional administrators, staff, and faculty should be keenly aware of the institution's policy with regard to external communication.

Thus, although a more loosely structured communication system is very appropriate for internal communications, a more tightly structured one is necessary for effective external communications.

MATRIX DESIGN

To overcome some of the problems of the classical chain of command structure of most organizations, including schools, matrix or mixed designs have evolved to improve mechanisms of lateral communication and information flow across the organization (Lewis, 1987).

The matrix organization, originally developed in the aerospace industry, is characterized by a dual authority system. There are usually functional and program or product line managers, both reporting to a common superior and both exercising authority over workers within the matrix. Typically, a matrix organization is particularly useful in highly specialized technological areas that focus on innovation. Thus, schools, school systems, and institutions of higher education make ideal settings for matrix designs. Especially in interdisciplinary academic programs, the matrix structure facilitates the coordination of the team and allows team members to contribute their special expertise.

The matrix design has some disadvantages that stem from the dual authority lines. Individual workers may find having two supervisors to be untenable, since it can create conflicting expectations and ambiguity. The matrix design may also be expensive as both functional and program managers may spend a considerable amount of time at meetings attempting to keep everyone informed of program activities. A matrix design in a college setting is depicted in **Figure 6.2**.

The use of matrix design in education is not very common, but it is a viable way of organizing when communication needs to occur outside the proper channels. The popularity of interdisciplinary and multicultural courses and programs in education has caused an increased interest in matrix design. Many high schools and colleges are informally organized in a matrix design. It would most likely serve these institutions well to consider it as a formal organizational structure, especially in cases when communication problems are evident.

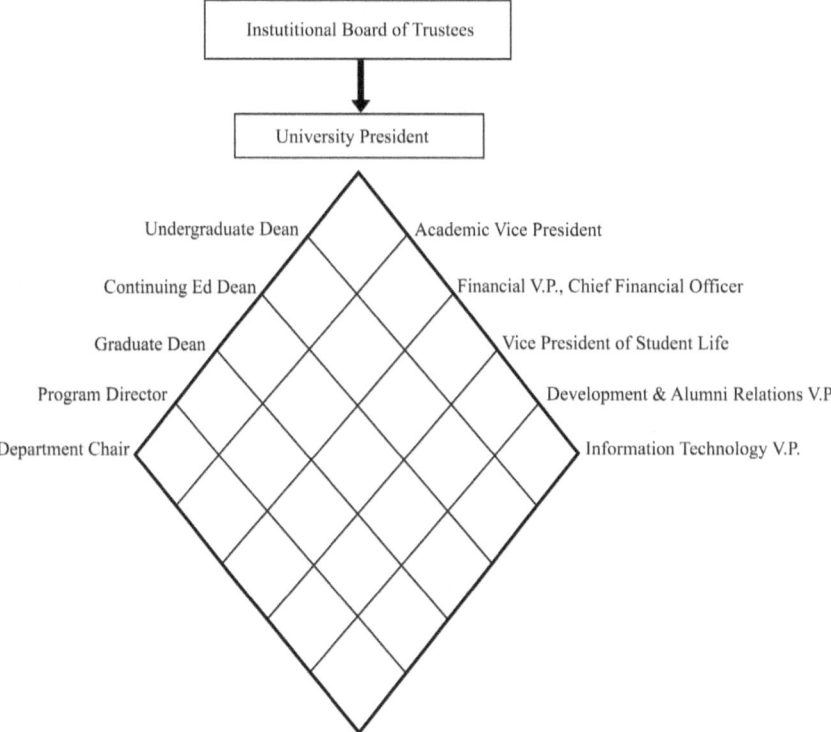

Figure 6.2. Matrix Design

CONCLUSION

Communication can single-handedly ensure absolute success or, alternatively, definitive demise. Consider the following:

> A foreign-born plumber in New York once wrote to the Bureau of Standards in Washington, DC, that he found hydrochloric acid an acceptable agent for cleaning drains, and he asked if they agreed. Washington replied, "The efficacy of hydrochloric acid is indisputable, but the chlorine residue is incompatible with metallic permanence." The plumber wrote back that he was mighty glad the bureau agreed with him. Considerably alarmed, the bureau replied a second time: "We cannot assume responsibility for the production of toxic and noxious residues with hydrochloric acid, and suggest you use an alternative procedure." The plumber was happy to learn the bureau still agreed with him, whereupon Washington wrote, "Don't use hydrochloric acid; it eats the hell out of pipes."

Communicating with ease and clarity is no simple task, and today's increasing reliance on digital communication in learning environments can make effective communication even more cumbersome. There are, however, various orientations toward how communication can be most effectively carried out.

Classical theory, social systems theory, and open systems theory (chapter 1) all incorporate a perspective toward the communication process, or who should say what through which channel to whom and to what effect. Classical theory stresses that the communication process exists to facilitate the manager's command and control over the employees in a formal, hierarchical, and downwardly directed manner. The purpose is to increase efficiency and productivity.

The social systems orientation suggests that, to be effective, communication has to be two way, and the meaning of the message is as much to be found in the psychological makeup of the receiver as it is the sender.

The open systems orientation emphasizes the communication process working toward drawing the various subsystems of an organization into a collaborating whole. Also, drawing the organization's actions into a close fit with the needs of its environment is an essential outcome of the process. This orientation emphasizes that the communication process must penetrate social class differences, cultural values, time orientations, and ethnocentrism of all types.

None of the conceptual frameworks, by itself, escapes the barriers to communication. The story of the plumber illustrates the problems of message coding, decoding, and transmission. It is suggested in order for communication to be effective, an adaptation of the process to the situation should be sought.

When communicating with the outside community, a more structured process may be appropriate; when communicating with the inside community, a less structured process might be more appropriate. This approach is in concert with one of the underlying themes of this book: whether speaking about organizational structure, leadership, motivation, or communication, it is necessary to adapt the approach or model to the situation. Taking a minute each day to obtain feedback regarding the effectiveness of the communication process at an institution is time well spent and will go a long way to ensuring a healthy organizational environment.

IMPLICATIONS FOR PRACTICE: SIGNIFICANCE OF COMMUNICATION CASE STUDY

Mx. Alex Grand, a newly hired director of facilities, is clearly a strong leader who sees the need for change. They bring a great deal of experience from a former job in which they institutionalized change, and they want to have it happen again.

However, the facility trades personnel, groundskeepers, and civil engineers under their purview are not clear as to what needs to be changed. They are unaware of Alex's vision for the department and how the institutionalization will affect them. Because Alex operates within a situational leadership style, they have confused and frustrated members of the department and are quickly setting up divisions within the facility team where unity had once reigned.

Alex's recent autocratic decisions regarding additional forms for tracking work orders and purchasing requests have angered the team, who already had a working process for these functions. They have also lengthened and completely revamped the structure of monthly department meetings. Meetings once scheduled for one hour now take three to four hours. In addition, now the staff is engaged in monthly service projects that seem to highlight Alex's perceived ineffectualness.

The Vroom-Yetton model of the decision-making process (see chapter 5) describes a stage in which the leader gathers information from subordinates, but does not necessarily tell them what the problem is, and then generates solutions in isolation. Alex favors engaging in this mode of decision-making.

As a central data-gathering process, shortly after their arrival to the university Alex began having informal chats with persons outside the facilities department, asking the person if they had ever had any problems with facilities and, if so, what was the problem. Alex believes these half-hour informal discussions provide enough information to act on without the facilities team ever knowing the details of the discussions. This practice has also prevented the facilities team from offering clarity or a rebuttal to the experience shared by external community members.

To date, no forum has been scheduled for the facilities team to learn of Alex's vision, nor has the facilities team been incorporated into decision-making processes. Many facilities members, if honest with themselves, would agree there is a need for some change, but they are not being given a chance to use their abilities to advance that change. There are many strong, able, experienced leaders within this vital campus department who are capable of igniting change in a positive way.

Still, Alex is quickly alienating the staff with their style of leadership. The staff remains unsure of Alex's direction for change, and the cost of their vision seems to be the loss of some of the staff's innate needs being met. Alex has taken away facilities team members' agency, power, and freedom, which had provided them with an internal locus of control under the previous administration.

Alex understands the importance of a collective, shared vision in order for institutional change to be successful. And, indeed, Alex believes they have been collaborative, open, and honest with the facilities team they lead.

Communication, like all aspects of leadership, should be contingent on the situation. Regrettably, in this situation, open communication is absent.

DIAGNOSTIC DEBRIEF

Here are some questions that may help in assessing an institution's communication process:

- How effective is the communication process?
- What barriers to communication exist?
- Is the correct communication style utilized under the proper conditions?
- Does communication include feedback where appropriate?
- Is there a climate of mutual trust and respect?
- Are active listening and other techniques that improve the communication process used?
- Do individuals use assertive, unassertive, or aggressive communication?

Chapter 7

Managing Conflict

> The quality of our lives depends not on whether or not we have conflicts, but on how we respond to them.
>
> —*Thomas Crum*

Everyone experiences conflict; it is unavoidable. Conflict is the result of incongruent or incompatible relationships, thoughts, behaviors, or decisions between and within individuals, groups, or organizations. Conflict can be public or private, formal or informal, rational or irrational. The likelihood of conflict increases when the parties have the chance to interact, when the parties see their differences as incompatible, and when there is a power differential between the parties that results in the dependence of one party on the other.

Most commonly, four circumstances are the result of conflict. First, when mutually exclusive goals or values actually exist or are perceived to exist by the groups involved, conflict can occur. In the collective bargaining process, for example, a trade union may perceive the administration's goals to be incompatible with those of the tradespersons and vice versa.

Another circumstance of conflict is when behavior is designed to defeat, reduce, or suppress the opponent. An example of this type of conflict often takes place in labor relations work. Specifically, unions and management have historically experienced conflict for this reason.

A symbiotic relationship based on interdependence is a third circumstance of conflict. This takes place when individuals or groups are dependent on one another. For example, if a foreign language professor does not follow the curriculum, the next-level instructor will be affected because the students will not have been properly prepared. In this example, the next-level professor might feel disenfranchised by the lack of student learning and skill development based on the negligent actions of the previous instructor.

The last commonly occurring conflict type occurs when each group attempts to create a relatively favored position. If the English department attempts to show administration it is superior to the other departments in the College of Arts and Sciences by demonstrating the others' ineptness, conflict occurs. Knowing these sources of conflict can go a long way toward precluding the surfacing of conflicts in the first place. A little preventive medicine, so to speak, is always in order.

Functionality or dysfunctionality can be an outcome of conflict. Effective administrators learn how to create functional conflict, prevent conflict from arising, and manage dysfunctional conflict when it does occur. They develop and practice techniques for diagnosing the causes and nature of conflict and transforming it into a productive force in the organization. Many colleges, for example, have a healthy competition between and among schools within the university for the recruitment of the most qualified students.

Some conflict is beneficial. It can encourage organizational change in the form of innovation, creativity, and adaption. For example, college robotic competitions allow schools to show off their advancements in STEM, engage students in applied-learning work, and foster innovation. The spirit of competition often spawns innovation in academic advancements and, more importantly, in curriculum and instruction for future student learning.

Interestingly, conflict can be viewed as dysfunctional for organizations. It can reduce productivity, decrease morale, cause overwhelming dissatisfaction, and increase tension and stress in the organization. It can arouse anxiety in individuals, increase the tension in an organizational system and its subsystems, and lower satisfaction. Production and satisfaction may decline; turnover and absenteeism may increase.

Avoidance, accommodation, compromise, competing/forcing, and collaborating are five behaviors or strategies administrators can utilize when conflict arises. Each style is appropriate to different situations that individuals or groups face in organizations. Once again, the underlying theme of contingency theory applies. These behaviors are illustrated in **Table 7.1**.

Table 7.1. Five Conflict Models

Conflict Handling Modes	Appropriate Situations
Competing	1. When quick, decisive action is vital—e.g., emergencies 2. On important issues where unpopular actions need implementing—e.g., cost cutting, enforcing unpopular rules, discipline 3. On issues vital to institutional welfare when you know you are right
Collaborating	1. To find an integrative solution when both sets of concerns are too important to be compromised 2. When your objective is to learn 3. To merge insights from people with different perspectives 4. To gain commitment by incorporating concerns into a consensus 5. To work through feelings that have interfered with a relationship
Compromising	1. When goals are important but not worth the effort or potential disruption of more assertive modes 2. When opponents with equal power are committed to mutually exclusive goals 3. To achieve temporary settlements to complex issues 4. To arrive at expedient solutions under time pressure
Avoiding	1. When an issue is trivial or more important issues are pressing 2. When you perceive no chance of satisfying your concerns 3. When potential disruption outweighs the benefits of resolution 4. To let people cool down and regain perspective 5. When gathering information supersedes immediate decision
Accommodating	1. When you find you are wrong—to allow a better position to be heard, to learn, and to show your reasonableness 2. When issues are more important to others than yourself—to satisfy others and maintain cooperation 3. To build social credits for later issues 4. To minimize loss when you are outmatched and losing 5. When harmony and stability are especially important

AVOIDANCE

When individuals or groups withdraw from a conflict situation, they act to satisfy neither their own nor the other party's concerns. Avoidance works best when individuals or groups face trivial or tangential issues, when they have little chance of satisfying their personal concerns, when conflict resolution will likely result in significant disruption, or when others can resolve the conflict more effectively. If two dorm roommates, for example, have an argument over sleeping arrangements (who gets the top bunk), the most appropriate strategy for managing the conflict may be avoidance. Let the students resolve the conflict in their own way and on their own terms.

In some circumstances, avoidance might be the right choice to manage conflict. Consider the proverbial story of the next-door neighbors whose children got into an argument and the adults tried to intervene on behalf of their respective children. The adults ended up being lifelong enemies, and the children were playing with each other again within the hour.

ACCOMMODATION

Sometimes called *diffusion*, accommodation can be used by individuals or groups. Accommodation demonstrates a willingness to cooperate in satisfying others' concerns while at the same time acting unassertively in meeting one's own.

Accommodating individuals often smooth over conflict. This mode builds social capital for later issues, results in harmony and stability, and satisfies others. An assistant director may capitulate on a disagreement with the director over a minor matter in hopes they can prevail on a larger issue in the future, thus building political and social capital for use in a future conflict. Again, accommodation can be an example of the age-old adage of losing a battle to win the war.

COMPROMISE

The compromise mode represents an intermediate behavior. It can include a sharing of positionality but not moving to the extremes. Hence, it often does not maximize the satisfaction of both parties. This style works well when goals are important but not sufficiently important for the individual or group to be more assertive, when the two parties have equal power, or when significant time pressure exists. For example, if two instructors in the same department disagree over what supplementary materials should be used for a certain lesson, they may compromise and use suggestions from each other collectively.

COMPETING/FORCING

Conflict in which competing or forcing is expressed finds one party trying to satisfy its own concerns while showing an unwillingness to satisfy the concerns of others. This strategy works well in emergencies, on issues calling for unpopular actions, in cases where one party is correct in its position, or where one party has much greater power. For example, if a sophomore undergraduate has suicidal ideation leading to a failed attempt, the dean of students may wish to inform the parents immediately and the psychological counselor may wish it to remain confidential. If the dean arbitrarily informs the parents immediately, they are using competing/forcing behavior.

COLLABORATING

Collaboration mode emphasizes problem solving with a goal of maximizing satisfaction for both parties, often resulting in a win/win solution. In practice this approach sees conflict as natural, showing trust and honesty toward others, and encouraging the airing of every person's attitudes and feelings. Each party exerts both assertive and cooperative behavior. Parties can use this mode when their objectives are to learn, to use information from diverse sources, and to find an integrative solution. If the trades union and the university agree to consider their differences to be a shared "our" problem rather than a "your" problem, both entities are taking a collaborative or problem-solving approach to resolve conflict.

One effective approach is, once one decides avoidance is not appropriate, to begin efforts toward conflict resolution with the collaborative mode. If this is not successful, one can move progressively toward compromise and accommodation, using force only as a last resort. During instances of high conflict and tension, it is important to be mindful of the role and interplay of both explicit and implicit bias (see chapter 2 for definitions of these terms) in collaborative processes.

IMPLICATIONS FOR PRACTICE: MANAGING CONFLICT CASE STUDY

More than 80 percent of the students at Prestige College are solidly upper middle class. Prestige has a strong academic profile and a reputation for quality education. Parental involvement in ancillary college functions frequently leads to parental influence on academic matters. Consequently, the college relinquishes its prerogative as purveyor of some decision-making.

Despite ample opportunities and resources to support learning, student discipline is the area of professional responsibility where Prestige College is most derelict. Codified institutional procedures are ignored in favor of a laissez-faire approach, permitting myriad inappropriate behaviors.

Attempts to gain control of the outside-of-the-classroom behaviors have led to increased parental complaints. Caregiver protests are given forum by an extremely political administration that disenfranchises college staff, especially those charged with adjudicating student discipline cases and officers responsible for ensuring safety within the college community. The general population of students at Prestige College believes that if they are involved in unruly or unsafe behaviors, it is unlikely they will face any serious disciplinary consequences.

This spring, necessary equipment, materials, and machinery for several upcoming summer renovation projects is being staged in a school parking lot. The area is sectioned off with yellow caution tape to prevent access and to ensure student safety. There are also public safety officials assigned to supervise this area (despite countless discussions concerning the effectiveness of public safety personnel presence).

Despite many factors contributing to these discussions, the college's public safety (PS) officers are not trained in effective management control. Collectively, they do not believe they have control (which students can sense immediately). Even though the officers go through de-escalation training, they hold no power to follow through on disciplinary actions.

In one past experience, officers and students ended up screaming at each other, with the students under the influence of alcohol and other banned substances. The students filed a formal complaint expressing their frustrations and blaming the PS officers. Rather than believing the officers on duty, who had no motive to fabricate stories of misbehavior, the parents overwhelmingly supported their children and redirected blame at the PS officers. The parents claimed the officers had yelled at their children for no reason.

It is now a week before the spring semester's end, and the seniors are on a particularly vengeful tear. They are jumping on top of one another, causing classmates to fall to the ground. Their behavior is creating a safety hazard. They have broken through the caution tape surrounding the construction site and are wrapping the brightly colored plastic around their necks and waists. What is even more appalling is the PS officers are present but neglect to take command.

DIAGNOSTIC DEBRIEF

Here are some questions that may help assess the conflict management capabilities of an institution:

- Is the conflict style in the institution functional or dysfunctional?
- Are preventive measures being employed to preclude conflict from occurring?
- Are there mechanisms for effectively managing conflict and stress?
- Does the use of these mechanisms reflect the situational nature of conflict resolution?
- Are avoidance, compromise, forcing, accommodation, and collaboration utilized in the appropriate situations?

Chapter 8

Directing with Power

> People who are truly strong lift others up. People who are truly powerful bring others together.
>
> —*Michelle Obama*

What is power? Power is the potential or actual ability to influence others in a desired direction. Who has the power in a situation? An individual, group, or other social unit has power if it controls information, knowledge, or resources desired by another individual, group, or social unit. Do different types of power exist? And if so, which type is more effective in organizational leadership? And finally, why is all this talk about power so important to educational leaders?

Answers to the aforementioned questions are examined in this chapter. Beginning with the reasons individuals or groups exert power, this chapter then examines the sources from which one derives power.

POWER IN THE ORGANIZATION

The value of identifying and using power behavior to improve individual and organizational performance is increasingly cited by organizational researchers, even calling its development and use the *central executive function* (see Kotter, 1978). Earlier views of power, stemming from coercion and corruption, have transformed as modern theorists and practitioners provide models and frameworks of power within an organization. Yet, although functional and advantageous in many situations, power behavior can also create conflict, which frequently is dysfunctional for the organization (Pfajfar et al., 2019; also see Kaplan, 1964).

ETHICAL ISSUES

How legitimate is the use of power in organizations? Certainly, if the use of power is manipulative and autocratic, it raises questions about the ethics of power. The abuse of power is evident not only in politics but also in schools, school districts, and institutions of higher education.

Administrators should establish guidelines for the ethical use of power in their institutions. They and other organizational members must emphasize its contribution to organizational effectiveness and control its abuses. Ensuring the rights of all organizational members are guaranteed is one criterion for its ethical use. This is especially appropriate in institutions that are not unionized, where the faculty and staff handbook should outline employee rights in a way similar to that of a labor agreement.

POWER AND DEPENDENCE

By estimating the extent of the dependence flowing in the opposite direction from power in a relationship, one can initially diagnose the level of power espoused by someone (Kotter, 1977). In other words, the power a parent has over their child is determined by the degree of dependence the child has on the parent.

Dependence arises in part because a person, group, or organization relies on another person, group, or organization to accomplish their or its tasks. A subordinate depends on their supervisor/leader for assistance in accomplishing a task and identifying obstacles to achieving a work goal. The person being relied or depended on automatically has some power to influence the other.

An academic provost, for example, might attempt to have the untenured faculty believe their continued employment depends largely on their support as a way to increase dependence on the provost. However, an untenured faculty member might circumvent the provost as much as possible to display independence from influence and to demonstrate agency.

EMPOWERING OTHERS

In most organizations, and certainly larger, more complex ones, leaders often relinquish some of their power. Task forces, whose membership reflects the makeup of the institution's community, are given either advisory or governance power in making decisions. This process empowers faculty and staff but ultimately enhances the power of the administration, because the organization is more likely to achieve its goals—and if it does, the administration looks good, which, in effect, increases administrator power.

SOURCES OF POWER

There are different ways of grouping or organizing sources of power. The preferred strategy consists of two larger categories: organizational and personal power. Under each of these categories are specific types of power.

Organizational Power

One's ability to influence the behavior of others within the organization is called *organizational power*. This is a broad category. Power is measured by the influence one has to get another stakeholder to comply with a request the stakeholder might otherwise oppose. Legitimate, reward, and coercive power fall under this power type.

Leaders who possess legitimate or positional power (as it is also referred to) can exert influence over others simply because of the authority associated with their job. This results in subordinates obeying the instructions given by a director, for example, simply by virtue of the position they hold.

In education, unions or the faculty tenure structure mitigate a president's legitimate power to a significant degree. Thus, it is inappropriate to rely on position as the only source of power. Interestingly, one study has found that as a supervisor's positional power increased, a subordinate's compliance increased, but the subordinate's satisfaction with supervision decreased (Rahim, 1989). This shows that the abuse of legitimate power can have diminishing returns.

Reward power (sometimes called resource power) is based on the notion that someone has control over resources or rewards that others within the organization want. Initially, reward power may be viewed with positive regard; however, the ability to withhold the reward for noncompliance is also a feature of this power type. Consider the senior financial administrator within a university. Their ability to control the allocation of fiscal resources may provide reward power for those who seek funding for special projects or interests.

Power can come from the control of scarce resources, such as money, materials, staff, or information. In an educational setting, financial officers, human resource leaders, and the provost often have reward power. Even information technology and communication personnel can possess resource power if demand for their services and time is considerably greater than the supply of these same resources.

Successfully motivating others through fear demonstrates harnessing coercive power. In the 2006 film *The Devil Wears Prada*, one of the main characters, Miranda Priestly, is depicted as a diabolical editor for a global fashion magazine. Miranda exerts coercive power, which influences subordinates to either cower when in her presence or to run in the opposite direction to avoid sharing space with her.

Coercive power can be very damaging in a workplace setting and has been linked to long-term traumatic stress for many who fall victim to its use. Transformative educational leaders would do well to refrain from using coercive power.

It is also important to consider the centrality of power. Specifically, power accrues to other positions because of their centrality. The more the activities of a position are linked and important to those of other individuals or subunits, the greater their centrality. A college president, for example, may have greater centrality than the board of trustees because the activities of more jobs are linked to the president than to the board. Thus, even though the board technically has more reward power, in reality, by way of centrality, the college president has more legitimate power.

Personal Power

When the knowledge or personality of an individual allows them to influence the behavior of others, they are said to harness personal power. Expert and referent power are subtypes of power under the personal power umbrella.

An individual who has unique or special knowledge, skills, and experience can use this expertise as a source of influence and as a way of building personal power. For example, when new innovative technology or learning devices are introduced into the market, the techie on the faculty often wields personal power based on their special knowledge and skills. In this scenario, expert power allows the tech-savvy faculty member to have influence over others.

As educational institutions and other organizations have become increasingly technology oriented, many technical support staff have acquired increased expert power within their organization. Admittedly, everyone has a super power, a specialized skill and/or area of knowledge in which they may be deemed an expert by peers. The goal is to channel this expertise to impact the way others think or behave.

Some people have an electric aura, a commanding presence, and/or a contagious personality. These individuals influence others because they have charisma or because others identify closely with shared values, beliefs, thoughts, or behaviors. This is called referent power.

An individual with charisma often exerts power because they attract others to follow. With this power type, others want to be associated with a specific individual; their inclination to follow a command or order is completely voluntary and not based on positional power. Often, when lateral dependence occurs among peers, it is the result of referent power based on an individual's charisma.

As previously mentioned, access to resources or information provides a source of influence under reward power. Another source of power often associated with reward power, but with less transience, is expertise. Expertise is more permanent than information-based power. For example, the first individuals to learn to use a new computer application might initially derive their power from having information others do not, but if their power persists even after the average user becomes digitally literate, personal power based on expertise has been obtained. Understandably, expert power is strongly associated with high performance and skill development.

SUMMARY

Power might be one of the least understood but most important areas of educational administration. This chapter described the sources and uses of power in institutions. Positional power, personal power, and resource- and information-based power were all described herein.

IMPLICATIONS FOR PRACTICE: DIRECTING WITH POWER CASE STUDY

Karina Jackson is the new vice president of human resources at Brooklyn University, and it is her first day on the job. As she reviews her daily schedule, she is reminded of the upcoming meeting that will take place immediately following the lunch hour. Karina will meet Lissa Willow, the custodial services union representative, for the first time.

Lissa's reputation as a direct, very assertive (borderline aggressive) administrator precedes her. Karina has already been forewarned of this impending encounter and has been given advice to present herself as a strong-willed individual who reached her position by aggressively pursuing professional goals. There's an air about the office that reeks of an intent to show dominance.

The scenario here is not unlike many that occur at educational institutions of all levels. This situation reflects the exercise of power in an organization.

What types of power might one expect to observe during this encounter at Brooklyn University? Recognizing, using, and dealing with power differences is implicit in negotiation, which is a process for reconciling different, often incompatible, interests of interdependent parties. At Brooklyn University, both Karina Jackson and Lissa Willow have power. How well each one uses her power and negotiation skills will determine her effectiveness.

DIAGNOSTIC DEBRIEF

Here are some questions that may be helpful in assessing the distribution of power in an institution:

- Is power appropriately shared?
- What type of negotiations occur in the school district or higher education institution, and do these negotiations tend to be distributive or integrative?
- What degree of preparation takes place to ensure contract language is understood by all?
- Are provisions made for the proper administration of the contract?

Chapter 9

Advancing with Strategy

Planning is bringing the future into the present so that you can do something about it.

—*Alan Lakein*

Organizational development experts concede that an effective leader must spend time developing goals and placing them in the context of a vision. There is a plethora of scholarly research that corroborates this recommendation, especially in educational settings. Several studies conclude that when institutions develop clear and agreed-upon goals that are duly promulgated, school effectiveness typically follows. Thus, successful administrators need to develop an educational vision that is mutually acceptable and understood by all components of the institution's community.

In some circles exactly what constitutes an educational vision seems to be shrouded in mystery. Actually, the process of developing an educational vision is not all that complex. The first step is to identify a list of broad goals. This step in the process should be done in conjunction with representatives from all components of the school community. Lack of sufficient representation from community members will lead to a lack of ownership among stakeholders, which can, in turn, jeopardize the successful implementation of a vision and goals.

The next step in the process is to merge and prioritize the goals and summarize them in the form of a short and concise statement. The following is an example of a vision statement:

> Empowering students to fulfill their academic, personal, and professional passions in a university that is diverse, oriented toward social justice, rich in history and culture, and inclusive of all students, faculty, and staff.

The key concepts in the above vision statement are "fulfill their academic, personal, and professional passions" and "diverse, oriented toward social justice, rich in history and culture, and inclusive of all." It is these concepts or goals a new educational leader would need to stress in all forms of communication and in all their interpersonal relations with the various internal and external institutional partners.

The final step is vision actualization, or the process known as *institutionalizing* the vision. This step ensures the vision statement endures even when the leadership of the institution changes. Operationalizing and placing the important concepts of the vision into the official policies and procedures of the school system is one important way of helping to institutionalize the educational vision and incorporate it into the school culture.

Another way of institutionalizing a vision is by encouraging the development of *heroes* who embody the institution's vision and *tribal storytellers* who promulgate it (Palestini, 2011). These are the individuals who are often described as "an institution around here."

Heroes such as these can do more to establish the organizational culture of an institution than manuals or a policies and procedures handbook could. The senior faculty member who is recognized and respected for their knowledge of the subject matter as well as their humane treatment of students is an invaluable asset to an educational institution. They symbolize and embody the vision through their actions and contributions.

It is the presence of heroes that sustains the reputation of the institution and allows the workforce to feel good about themselves and about where they work. The deeds and accomplishments of these heroes need to be narrated. Their stories and contributions need to become part of the folklore of the institution.

The deeds of these heroes are usually perpetuated by the tribal storytellers within an organization. These individuals know the history of the organization and relate it through stories of its past and present heroes. Knowing they provide an invaluable service to the institution, an effective leader encourages the work of tribal storytellers.

Storytellers contribute to the process of institutional renewal; they allow the institution to continuously improve. Through their narrated stories, they preserve and revitalize the values of the institution. They also mitigate the tendency of institutions, especially educational institutions, to become bureaucratic. Every institution has heroes and storytellers. It is the educational leader's responsibility to ensure things like manuals and handbooks do not replace their institutional legends.

A STRATEGIC PLANNING PROCESS FOR EDUCATIONAL INSTITUTIONS

Once a vision statement is crafted and adopted through a collaborative and iterative process, it is time to consider establishing a strategic plan. Components of a strategic plan can vary, but below are ten activities that should be considered for inclusion in a strategic plan for educational institutions:

1. ***Develop a mission statement.*** The process of developing a mission statement involves establishing a strong group consensus about the unique purposes of the educational institution and its place in the community it serves. The process of developing the mission will set the tone for all further planning activity. Most often, educational institutions have an existing mission. However, the planning process should not begin until either there is broad acceptance of the current mission or the mission is revised or rewritten. Many times, the mission needs to be revised to adapt to current circumstances before the process can continue. Mission statements are meant to be dynamic, not static.

   The educational vision of the school is derived from the mission statement. It is often a concise summary of the mission or how one expects the mission to play out for the future.

2. ***Develop a set of institutional goals.*** The institution should next develop a set of goals it deems appropriate in the accomplishment of its mission. Goals are more specific and give direction to the action that needs to take place to achieve them. The goals should be expressed in terms that would promote easy assessment. It should be clear to an objective observer whether they have been achieved. An example of a goal that could be derived from the mission statement listed earlier would be, "To provide an education that addresses all dimensions of a student's character—mental, psychological, physical, and spiritual."

3. ***Develop learning outcome statements.*** The process of developing student learning outcome statements, including transitional outcomes, should include the outcomes students must achieve in order to meet the institutional goals and progress from one level to the next. An example of a typical outcome statement might be, "Upon completing two general education program courses in a foreign language, the student will have the ability to speak conversationally with a native speaker of the language."

   Ways of authentically assessing these educational outcomes also need to be developed. The current emphasis on outcomes-based learning, authentic assessment, and measurable growth focuses quite heavily on this step in the planning process.

4. ***Establish stakeholder groups.*** Following the previous step, in which outcome statements were drafted, a group of internal and external stakeholder groups are solicited to provide important, critical feedback. This step helps ensure the collection of unique and distinct perspectives from a variety of constituency groups. Accepting a wide range of perspectives provides for more robust sharing and understanding of the outcomes as they relate to different interests. Transparency of the planning process, goals, and outcomes comes as a result of internal and external stakeholder involvement. Lastly, this step provides outreach for extended community engagement from neighbors, local business owners, parents, civic and municipal leaders, and other stakeholders.

5. ***Develop the curriculum.*** The essence of a plan is to ensure the learning organization is growing to meet the developing needs of students. Because current students enrolling in post-secondary education have different academic needs than those who came before them, educational institutions must also evolve. Consider a general education program—a set of foundational courses (typically at liberal arts schools) students are required to take—in which the courses are developed to include a number of the learning outcomes determined earlier. Planning should ensure all of the learning outcomes have been incorporated into at least one of the courses.

6. ***Conduct a comprehensive needs analysis.*** A needs analysis is a crucial part of the strategic planning process. It must involve a comprehensive identification of both internal and external strengths and weaknesses and include an analysis of instructional practices. The process should rely on both quantitative and qualitative data.

    A needs analysis should involve all stakeholder groups within the local community, giving each an opportunity to provide both hard data and informed opinion. Methods for data gathering for a comprehensive needs analysis may include any or all of the following: gap analysis, landscape scanning, competitor benchmarking, and a formal SWOT (strengths, weaknesses, opportunities, and threats) analysis. The result of the needs analysis should be the main tool in developing priority goal areas for action planning.

7. ***Develop a list of priorities.*** Priorities are identified by a process that applies the information accumulated during the needs analysis to the list of general institutional goals identified earlier. Goals that show a need for developmental action are prioritized on the basis of their relationship to the identified mission and on the severity of the need.

Topic: Increase Business Student preparedness through course offerings and mastering effective communication.

- **Goal 1:** Prepare students to meet and exceed writing expectations in the job application process and in the professional world.
  - **Objective A:** Modify Business Communication assignments so students better match the requirements expected in the professional context.
  - **Metric #1:** An increase from 50% to 75% in the percentage of Business students receiving interviews in the on-campus recruitment process after submitting their cover letters within the year after the requisite changes to course assignments and rubrics are implemented. *This metric would show students' cover letters are increasing in effectiveness.*
  - **Resources:** The resources required to implement this goal include: two summer stipends of $4,000 each, two non-tenure-track faculty lines at $110,000/year w/fringe benefits, one staff position at $55,000/year with fringe benefits, and approximately fifteen hours per person over the course of a semester from each of the Business Communication Center's seven full-time assistant professors. Training and materials total $25,000 per year for the entire department staff. The estimated overall annual cost for this goal is $269,800.
  - **Annual Expense Resources**

Item	Quantity	Item Cost	Fringe Benefits*	Total Cost
Summer Stipends	2	$4,000	$0	$8,000
Non-tenure Track Faculty	2	$65,000	$18,200	$166,400
Admin Position	1	$55,000	$15,400	$70,400
Training & Materials	1	$25,000	$0	$25,000

*(Calculated based on 28% of Salary)

Total:	$269,800

Figure 9.1. Strategic Planning Goal/Objective/Metric/Resource Alignment

8. ***Develop specific action plans.*** One or more action plans or strategies are developed for each of the priority goal areas. The action plans identify specific actions to be taken to meet the identified priority needs. **Figure 9.1** provides an example of an action plan. Action plans typically include the following items:
   a. Topic—a major strategy to be completed
   b. Goal(s)—typically begins with an action verb
   c. Objectives—typically two or three per goal

d. Metrics/assessment/evaluation process—a finite plan to measure the success of the goal and objectives
e. Resources—estimated service and product costs for enacting the plan
f. Projected timelines or completion dates—**Figure 9.2** shows a timeline for a strategic plan
g. The person or group responsible

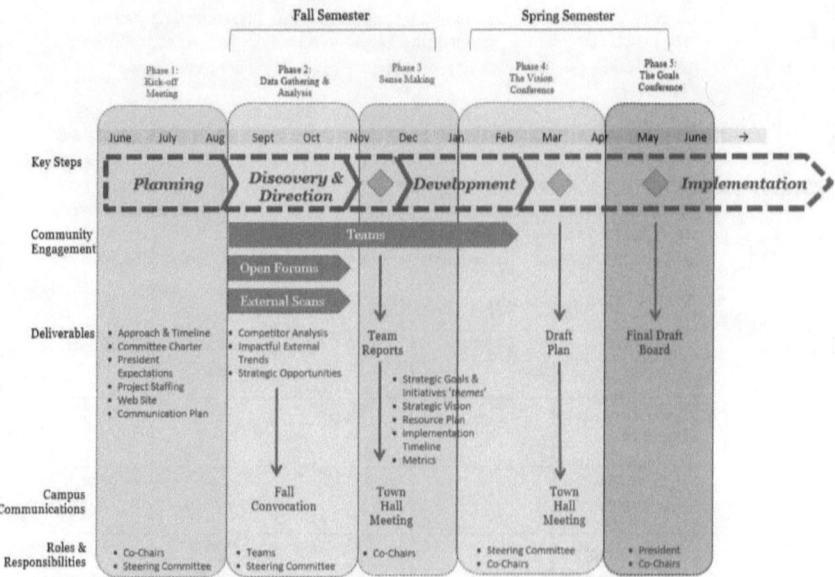

Figure 9.2. Timeline for a Strategic Plan

9. *Develop an assessment plan.* The assessment plan ascertains the degree to which the student learning outcomes are achieved. The assessment plan should include the following:
   a. The general purpose of the assessments
   b. A description of the process to be used to develop and analyze portfolios of student work, including a variety of strategies
   c. A description of assessment procedures to be used
   d. A description of how the assessment results will be used
   e. A description of how the institution will assist students who have not demonstrated mastery of the outcomes
   f. A description of the process for notifying stakeholders of assessment results
10. *Prepare a professional development plan.* The final step in the academic planning process is to prepare a professional development plan to train and prepare the staff to implement the plans. This step is especially

important if new and innovative approaches are required to implement the strategic plan.

STRATEGIC PLANNING MODELS

The previous ten-step process provides a fairly common approach used in educational environments. These steps may be modified or reordered to meet the needs and preferences of the organization. There are also other models that some organizations may choose to follow. The sections below provide context for two specific models: Bryson's (2018) ABCs of strategic planning and Sanaghan's (2009) collaborative strategic planning process.

ABCs of Strategic Planning

Planning for the future is a vital function for organizations. A popular method used for gathering data, analyzing possibilities and challenges, and determining a pathway for success is the development of a strategic plan (often called a *comprehensive* plan in K-12 settings). Bryson (2018) defines strategic planning as "a deliberative, disciplined effort to produce fundamental decisions and actions that shape and guide what an organization (or other entity) is, what it does, and why it does it." This definition informs the three-step process outlined in the model.

Bryson offers a three-part model for organizations to follow when creating a strategic plan: (1) vision, mission, and goals; (2) strategy formulation; and (3) strategy implementation.

The ABCs of strategic planning is a model that employs a targeted question and tools to guide organizations from one component of the model to the next. For example, asking the questions "Where are you?" and "Where do you want to be?" leads to vision, mission, and goal development. Strategy formulation takes place in the space between "where you are" and "how to get there." Finally, strategy implementation is created when organizations explore "how to get there" and "where you want to be."

Gathering stakeholders to vet answers to the three principle questions lays the foundation for goal development. After goals are determined, organizational leaders meet to develop objectives, or action statements, that support work toward goal accomplishment. Finally, goal metrics and resources needed for plan implementation are determined.

To offer an example, a strategic planning goal might be "To enrich academic quality and distinction." This goal would then be supported by several objectives, such as "Develop and support new teaching spaces and cutting-edge facilities" and "Implement a new inclusive instructional model."

Measurable metrics for the goal's objectives must then be created. In the aforementioned example, a metric for the first objective might be the creation of a campus master plan that will be used to address facility renovation needs.

Resources needed for this metric would include allocated funds to hire an architectural firm to assist with the creation of a master plan. A finished comprehensive plan commonly has four to six major goals with two to four objectives under each goal.

Collaborative Strategic Planning

Different from the ABCs model of strategic planning, Sanaghan (2009) provides a unique framework for consideration. This model seeks high engagement and inclusion from multiple stakeholders in order for the planning process to be efficient and effective in its execution.

A key component of Sanaghan's process is the creation of a highly credible internal planning task force (PTF), which is given responsibility for steering the organization through the entire collaborative process. Acting as a change agent, the PTF "taps into and builds the capacity of the institution to think and plan in collaborative and inclusive ways" (Sanaghan, 2009). Throughout the entire planning process, stakeholders are given a voice and remain active in plan development activities.

Aside from the collaborative nature of this model, an additional value that must be maintained is transparency. Opportunities for sharing and seeking feedback are maintained throughout plan development as a way of enhancing stakeholder buy-in and ensuring plan transparency. In the end, this framework grants maximum stakeholder involvement and contribution, allowing for the creation of a robust future trajectory for the organization.

As its name suggests, this model gives great intentionality to collaboration. The overall framework is outlined in a multiphase linear process. The phases are (1) getting organized, (2) data gathering, (3) sensemaking, (4) vision conference, and (5) goals conference.

1. In the first phase, organizational leadership widely communicates the purpose of the strategic planning process to garner enthusiasm and stakeholder interest. This is also the phase in which the PTF is established. In this phase the organizational leader also confirms their role as a planning process champion, but not a driver or controller of the development of the plan; these roles are reserved for the PTF.
2. The data gathering and engagement phase of this model is considered one of the most crucial. Within this phase, the PTF engages in meaningful discussions and dialogue with as many different and diverse stakeholder groups as possible. The PTF is also provided training that

includes activities designed to ensure lots of cross-sectional involvement and engagement. Data-gathering work is completed through face-to-face engagement, interviews, focus groups, and survey data collection techniques.

3. In the sensemaking phase, the PTF meets to review all the data that was collected in phase two. Sifting through this mountain of data, they conclude their deliberations with a series of authored concept papers. These papers offer a brief and concise description of major themes determined as a result of analyzing all available and relevant data. Once written and reviewed by others in the PTF, the concept papers are then made public and are circulated to all members of the organization.

4. Next, a one-day, highly interactive meeting called the visions conference is held. This workshop brings together between fifty and seventy stakeholders from both internal and external groups. There are three functions that take place at the visions conference. First, participants review and discuss the concept papers written by the PTF. Stakeholders are then divided into smaller groups and asked to discuss and share from their unique perspective important ideas for the future direction of the organization. Creating a preferred future is the last task of the visions conference. Still working in smaller groups, stakeholders are asked to frame their future vision for the organization into a five-year framework. They then give formal presentations to the entire conference audience.

   Facilitated discussions after the presentations help identify common ground themes that are then written into a drafted vision statement for the organization. This is shared and distributed to all stakeholders within the organization.

5. The last phase of the collaborative strategic planning process is the goals conference. The PTF convenes for a one- or two-day working meeting to create a broad plan for implementation. The vision statement and concept papers are referenced to establish goals and strategic themes. Action plans are then drafted for each identified goal. Following the goals conference, the action plans are sent to organizational leaders for discussion and review. Once approved, the plan is published in its final copy and distributed widely. In many cases, leaders who will oversee the implementation of various goals have been identified from their participation in the visions conference or previous planning engagement activities.

SUMMARY

A strategic plan is a guide grounded in mission to identify core values that inform the vision and alignment toward established immediate and long-term objectives. It defines measurable priorities, action plans, for internal and external stakeholders that demonstrate a commitment to organizational growth and momentum toward future goals.

This chapter outlines common steps employed by organizations when developing a comprehensive plan. In addition, two specific frameworks are shared with the readership. Both Bryson's (2018) ABCs strategic planning process and Sanaghan's (2009) collaborative strategic planning process provide differentiated methodologies for consideration in the development of an organization's future plan.

IMPLICATIONS FOR PRACTICE: ADVANCING WITH STRATEGY CASE STUDY

Nestled in the Missouri flatlands are two of the few remaining single-sex institutions in the American higher education landscape. Bradford College is a school for men. Addison College educates women. For both colleges, the hierarchical structure of the board of trustees, institutional leadership, and alumni donors have precluded each college from making decisions such as whether to become coeducational.

As premier colleges, both have a long-standing history of transforming their students through rigorous scholarly pursuits, engagement in collegiate athletics, and strong fraternity and sorority memberships. In addition, each school has benefited from its adjacent campus location. For the last ten years, the colleges' strong partnership has developed to allow students to take a limited number of elective courses on the other's campus. Students have also enjoyed jointly attending programming events, guest lectures, and social activities. Despite such comradery, their single-sex historical roots run deep and until now have never been questioned.

Faced with an unexpected quandary, preluded by declining enrollment, diminishing federal and alumni funding, and competing resources, three weeks ago Bradford College and Addison College announced the merging of their schools beginning next fall. As a normative experience of American higher education for more than a century, the conceptual creation of coeducation is not novel. However, it is difficult for many college leaders, faculty, staff, alumni/alumnae, and students to imagine what coeducation means for these two colleges.

Despite the apprehensions of stakeholders, Dr. Jones, president of Bradford College, and Dr. Smith, president of Addison College, remain realistically concerned yet deeply committed to their future transition. They realize they will need a strategic plan to help both institutions successfully merge into one united entity.

DIAGNOSTIC DEBRIEF

Here are a few questions that can assess an institution's understanding and commitment to its goals:

- Does a mission statement exist? Does it accurately reflect the current aspirations of the organization?
- Does a vision statement exist? Does it need to be amended?
- Does a strategic plan exist? If yes, which goals have been achieved and which ones remain?
- Are the goals, objectives, and strategies clear and measurable?
- Are they known and understood by the school community?
- Is the planning process ongoing?

Chapter 10

Leadership Through Transition

> I alone cannot change the world, but I can cast a stone across the water to create many ripples.
>
> —*Mother Teresa*

Challenges facing education in general, and higher education specifically, are plentiful. In American higher education, stagnant and declining enrollments, increased costs of tuition, limited financial resources, and outdated physical spaces plague many institutions. Such pitfalls have led to an increase in partnerships with private markets and a rise in institutional acquisitions and mergers.

In many cases, the need for change is imminent, yet resistance to change remains resolute. Despite its difficulty, the process of change is absolutely necessary if an organization is to continually improve. Thus, to be an effective leader, especially in the transformational style, an administrator must become a change agent and master the processes that can bring change about effectively.

AN INTEGRATED APPROACH TO CHANGE

The organizational literature is replete with various suggested change processes. Many of them contain helpful components leading to successful transformation, but few contain all of the necessary elements. As a result, through the process of trial and error, the following recommendations have been developed regarding the process for change. The name, *integrated change process*, is fitting as there are distinct steps in this process, yet the key to their successful implementation is simultaneous rather than sequential implementation.

In an earlier work, entitled *Ten Steps to Educational Reform: Making Change Happen*, the following steps in the process are suggested (Palestini, 2000):

- Establish a climate for change
- Assess the need for change
- Create a sense of urgency
- Assess favorable and opposing forces
- Select from the alternatives
- Promote ownership
- Provide professional development
- Operationalize the change
- Evaluate the change
- Institutionalize the change

When educational leaders neglect to formally plan and do not fully engage in all the steps in the change process, reform efforts typically fail. Failures can also occur when administrators try to implement reform by following the change process steps sequentially rather than simultaneously. This can lead to lingering in one of the steps, unable to bring the process to closure.

Whether it be an apparently insignificant change, such as deciding between the homogenous or the heterogeneous grouping of students (tracking) or what form of assessment should be used in course selection, or a more significant reform, such as whether state aid should be given to private educational institutions, the integrated implementation of these steps will help bring about the desired change.

ESTABLISH A CLIMATE FOR CHANGE

Hanson (1991), in his text entitled *Educational Administration and Organizational Behavior*, describes an incident regarding the process of change. Always interested in the processes of school improvement, he once asked an educational leader, "How does change come about around here?" She thought for a moment. "Well," she replied, "there is the normal way and the miraculous way. The normal way," she continued, "is where the heavens part and the angels come down and do the change for us. The miraculous way is when we do it ourselves."

If one has established a climate of change at their institution, change will come to be expected. It will be perceived as something positive and routine. The need for change in the context of continuous improvement should be articulated constantly by institutional leaders.

College presidents, provosts, and administrative leaders should set the tone for change by taking every opportunity to articulate its necessity and model it in their own leadership. For example, faculty convocations can be opportunities to articulate the notion that if the institution is to progress, academically and operationally, it must be open to change. At the initial meeting, the possible changes that are anticipated during the upcoming academic year can be shared. At subsequent faculty meetings, the need for change can be reinforced.

In addition to articulating the need for change, to promote a positive organizational climate the leader must model a tolerance for change. Even in low-risk decisions, such as changing the color of the library walls or modifying the format of faculty meetings to incorporate innovative concepts like community-based learning and shared decision-making, the leader needs to lead by example. The leader must be perceived as being open to new ideas and must provide a climate in which creativity is fostered. In other words, leaders must model the change they expect in others.

If a positive climate for change is to be established, another requisite is an environment of trust and respect. Arguably, the most valuable resource within an organization is its people, the individuals most influential in making an institution successful. The very best educators and administrators can work anywhere they please; they have choices. Educational leaders who treat all employees with the respect and appreciation with which they treat volunteers are poised for greatness.

NEEDS ASSESSMENT

Completing a needs assessment is the next step in the integrated change process. Unfortunately, this step is often ignored. Many educational leaders become enamored with one educational reform or another and try to implement it whether or not there is an identified and agreed-upon need. Reforms are often adopted arbitrarily by misguided educational administrators. When implemented without a needs assessment, these changes are almost always destined to fail.

Ordinarily, a needs assessment calls for a review of existing data and may require some surveying of the various components or stakeholders of the educational community. A certain amount of risk is always present when completing a needs assessment. In the process of uncovering needs, one might also raise expectations that all respondent concerns will be prioritized and addressed.

Fundamental to effecting change is priority setting and focus; thus, not all needs can be met immediately. Resources are in short supply. Difficult and sometimes painful decisions have to be made whereby some crucial needs will not be met or given the attention they deserve. Three reference groups are especially important to the needs assessment and the change process: students and parents, professional staff, and educational policy makers. Often it is the students and/or parents who are left out of the process. Leaving them out, of course, has implications for distribution of power and motivation, and empirical research suggests it is much better to include rather than exclude key stakeholders.

Data about students are readily available in the records a typical educational institution generates and maintains. Course grades, judicial records, financial records, percentage of students with disabilities, transportation reports, and a host of other official and unofficial data serve as sources for developing a profile of the students enrolled at the institution. Informal discussions with colleagues, other professionals, and the students and parents themselves are another source of information. Student focus groups and systematic observation by both faculty and administrators are other ways of assessing whether there is a need for change.

Local and state educational board members, state departments of education, legislators, the US Department of Education, and education advocacy groups should also be consulted to identify the needs of an educational institution. Lastly, the reports of accrediting agencies, such as the Middle States Association, Phi Beta Kappa, the American Association of Colleges and Schools of Business, and the Society of College and University Planning, just to name a few, can be valuable resources for assessing the needs of an institution.

CREATE A SENSE OF URGENCY

Because often there is a natural instinct to resist change, a sense of alarm or urgency must be created to effect change. The change agent must articulate the dire consequences of remaining in the status quo in order to overcome the innate sense of inertia.

There are a number of ways to create a sense of urgency, including citing comparable data from similar institutions and projected student enrollment declines. But in creating a sense of urgency, the change agent must be aware that individuals and groups are often moved by dissimilar forces. In other words, what might cause a sense of urgency in one person might cause a sense of hopelessness in another, which in turn can lead to a self-fulfilling prophecy.

Thus, creating a sense of urgency or stress can have both functional and dysfunctional outcomes. Whether stress takes a constructive or destructive course is influenced by the sociocultural context in which the stress occurs. A culture of trust and respect is a considerable asset.

Effective educational leaders learn how to create functional conflict and manage dysfunctional conflict. They develop and practice techniques for diagnosing the causes and nature of stress and transform them into a productive force that fosters needed change in the institution.

ASSESS FAVORABLE AND OPPOSING FORCES

Perhaps the most important step in the integrated change process is accurate assessment of the forces that affect proposed change. Correctly identifying the forces that favor reform and those opposing it is crucial to the effective implementation of change. Furthermore, interventions chosen to neutralize forces against change, and those selected to enhance forces in favor of transformation, are instrumental to the eventual success of the integrated change process.

Forces resistant to change can be considerable. These forces range from simple ignorance to complex vested interests. This brings about an awareness that the enemy may be the very people involved in or leading the change process.

Identifying forces resistant to change is an important part of transforming the organization's environment or culture. These forces must be diagnosed, understood, and considered in the targeting process and in selecting a change strategy. A major organizational feature that contributes to resistance to change is the domestication of educational institutions (Carlson, 1990). A domesticated organization has many properties of a monopoly: it does not have to compete for resources, except in a very limited area; it has a steady flow of clients; and its survival is guaranteed.

Although some educational institutions do not possess all the same domesticating characteristics, many faculty, administrators, and staff view their institutions in this way. One often hears the college professor or athletic coach proclaim in the light of declining enrollments, "That's the administration's problem." The ability to reframe single-view ownership over critical issues can be helpful in creating a plan to transform community members to understand their place and influence in enacting change across the institution, even in areas that are seemingly outside their purview.

FORCE-FIELD ANALYSIS

To understand the shifting forces affecting a change, leaders can use an analytical technique called force-field analysis, which views a problem as a product of forces working in different, often opposite, directions. An organization, or any of its subsystems, maintains the status quo when the sum of opposing forces is zero. When forces in one direction exceed forces in the opposite direction, the organization or subsystem moves in the direction of the greater forces. For example, if forces for change exceed forces against change, then change is likely to occur. This notion is credited to Lewin (1951) but remains prominent in the work of contemporary scholars.

To move the educational institution toward a different desired state requires increasing the forces *for* change, decreasing the forces *against* change, or both. Generally, reducing resistance forces creates less tension in the system and fewer unanticipated consequences than increasing forces for change.

Suppose an institution is moving from homogenous to heterogeneous enrollment (a.k.a. moving from a single-gender to coeducational institution). Reducing the resistances to the changes created by the introduction of heterogeneous grouping increases the likelihood of the changeover. When the administrators and staff no longer resist change, the present state moves closer to the desired state.

In the example of heterogeneous grouping, moving from homogenous grouping in the form of tracking to the more egalitarian heterogeneous grouping is bound to encounter resistance. What are the opposing forces one can anticipate? Certainly, some of the alumni will be against the change because the institution will develop a new culture and identity different from the one they experienced as an undergraduate.

On the contrary, what are the forces in favor of change? Once again, one can anticipate certain alumni will favor the more inclusive approach embodied in heterogeneous enrollment. A savvy administrator will be able to apply interventions that would neutralize the opposition and mobilize the forces in favor of this change. Using force-field analysis in a systematic way can be very helpful in bringing about desired change (see **Figure 10.1**).

DEVELOP AND SELECT ALTERNATIVES

While the already-mentioned steps in the integrated change process are being addressed, the change agent should establish a committee or task force of *believers* to begin developing alternatives that would address the perceived need(s). Ideally, a deliberative consideration of the various alternatives

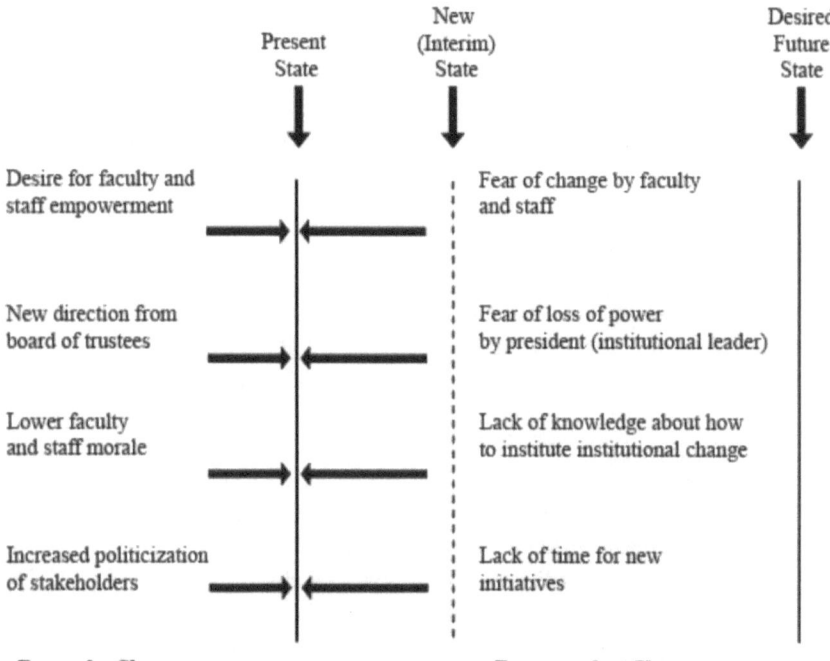

Figure 10.1. Force-Field Analysis

should be undertaken, and the ones that best satisfy the cost/benefit analysis should be chosen. All too often, however, those with power have arbitrarily chosen their preferred alternative, and the change agent is expected simply to implement it.

Another phenomenon that sometimes occurs during this phase of the change process is the tendency to satisfice, or choose the alternative that offends the fewest individuals and/or groups rather than choose the best alternative. *Satisficing* is a term coined by Herbert Simon, a Nobel Prize winner in economics, who was critical of the so-called rational model of decision-making, which indicates decision makers develop and analyze all of the possible alternatives and select the best one available (Simon, 1960).

At a certain point in the decision-making process, rather than choose the best possible alternative, in the interest of efficiency the decision maker will give concession, or sacrifice the optimal solution or alternative for one that is satisfactory or adequate. For example, if an academic dean is trying to decide between traditional place-based (face-to-face) instruction versus online instruction, the change agent may satisfice and choose an integrated hybrid model that combines what is believed to be the best aspects of both modalities.

Thus, the change agent may sacrifice the optimal solution for one that satisfies the greatest number of constituencies.

PROMOTE A SENSE OF OWNERSHIP

It is a truism that if a change is to be implemented successfully in education, it must have the support and acceptance of the faculty and staff. In simple terms, people take part in things they help create. Asserting a sense of ownership is a tried-and-true way to increase personal accountability. Still, how does a leader effectively promote employee ownership? An answer to this question is provided in the following four suggested steps:

1. ***Respect people.*** As was earlier indicated, a culture of respect starts with appreciating the diverse gifts individuals bring to the organization. The key is to dwell on the strengths of coworkers rather than on their weaknesses or areas in need of improvement.
2. ***Let values guide policy and practice.*** Developing a culture of civility in an institution was previously mentioned as an important aspect of a strong learning environment. If there is an environment of mutual respect and trust, the institution will flourish. Leaders need to let the organization's value system guide behavior and action. Style is merely a consequence of what is believed and what is in the hearts of those occupying the space.
3. ***Recognize the need for covenants.*** Contractual agreements cover such things as salary, fringe benefits, and working conditions. They are part of organization life, and there is a legitimate need for them. Seen as an element of trust and not a lack thereof, covenantal relationships provide protection and power. Workers choose their employers—and they usually choose where they work—based on reasons less tangible than salaries and fringe benefits. Covenantal relationships enable educational institutions to be civil, hospitable, and cognizant of individuals' differences and unique natures.
4. ***Understand that culture counts more than structure.*** An educational institution recently went through a particularly traumatic time when the credibility of the administration was questioned by the faculty and staff. Various organizational development consultants were interviewed to facilitate a healing process. Most of the consultants spoke of making the necessary structural changes to create a culture of trust. The consultant who was hired, however, began with the attitude that organizational structure has nothing to do with building trust. Interpersonal relations

based on mutual respect and an atmosphere of goodwill is what creates a trusting culture.

PROVIDE STAFF DEVELOPMENT

Staff development, while an essential part of the change process, is often neglected or overlooked completely. Many educational reforms have failed because of an enthusiastic but ill-advised leader who has tried to implement a change before engaging in staff development.

Sometimes, even when staff development is provided, the quality of the training is poor. Negative responses to staff development are often the result of a history of poor experiences with such activities. Still, the answer is not to eliminate their occurrence. Rather, an astute leader will respond by ensuring the next professional development opportunity is worthwhile.

As has been mentioned, the most important resource in an institution is its people. When employees are congruent on organizational needs, and when they are well trained, adaptive, and motivated, effective transformation results. To achieve this goal requires attention to the various ways in which human potential can be realized. It also calls on a variety of needs any particular person or group might have at any particular stage of development. Providing adequate and effective staff development enables individuals to reach their potential; it enables them to succeed.

OPERATIONALIZE CHANGE

At this point in the integrated change process, operationalization of the change takes place, or gives form to a vision. Although careful preparation for change increases the chances of success, it does not guarantee effective action. Placing the plan in operation requires the establishment of the organizational structure that will best suit the change, and development of an assessment process to determine if the change is remaining on course.

Briefing sessions, special seminars, or other means of information dissemination must permeate the change effort. Operationalizing the change must include procedures for keeping all participants informed about the change activities and their effects. Transparency is key to the operationalization process. Technology can be helpful through the use of shared electronic files for this cause.

EVALUATE CHANGE

Assessing change is the next step in the integrated change process. Authentic assessment is a topical issue in education these days. Many are questioning exactly how to assess performance and student growth most accurately, effectively, and fairly. After generations of focusing on program inputs, stressing program *outcomes* as an authentic measure of a program's effectiveness is gaining in popularity. An emphasis on outcomes versus inputs is much preferred in assessing the true effectiveness of a change or reform.

The change agent should collect data about the nature and effectiveness of the change. The results of the evaluation indicate whether the change process is complete or should return to an earlier stage. The criteria for success should be specified in advance of a change effort. These criteria can be culturally linked and varied; they also should be closely related to the *goals* of the reform.

If ineffective outcomes result from the introduction of a new general education curriculum model, for example, the process should return to an earlier stage, such as needs assessment, to determine if the institution is really in need of it and if the educational community has been properly prepared.

INSTITUTIONALIZE CHANGE

Provided the evaluation process shows reform has been effective, the change then should become institutionalized—that is, the changed processes and/or programs should be established as permanent ways of operating. Otherwise, when the current change agent leaves, the change may not be perpetuated.

In ideal circumstances, reform should become part of the organizational culture. It is in this way that a legacy is created from which future generations of students, faculty, administration, and staff can benefit. The results of a failure to institutionalize change are often seen at the state and federal Department of Education levels. How many times has a US governor or president set an effective educational agenda, only to have it scuttled and replaced with a different agenda by the subsequent administration? If a successful change is to prevail over time, it must be institutionalized.

Educational leaders, therefore, must build learning communities, ones that emphasize ongoing adaptability and self-generation, nurture agility in response to change and ambiguity, and harness creativity and innovation in opposition to stagnation. Peter Senge (1990) says, "Leaders in learning organizations are responsible for building organizations where people are continually expanding their capabilities to shape their future—that is, leaders are responsible for learning." Where better to implement the idea of learning communities than in an educational institution?

CONCLUSION

Healthy organizations are ones that are continually improving (Deming, 2000). Continuous improvement assumes change. Therefore, if an educational leader is to be effective, they must become an agent of change.

Mastering the change process requires a leader to know and understand the steps involved in planning a successful transformation in an organization. If change can take place in an atmosphere of mutual trust and respect, its chances for success are maximized.

Ascertaining the need for change from those within the organization is a suggested model for effecting reform. Then, transformational leaders should diagnose forces influencing change for the purpose of implementing initiatives that maximize the forces in favor of reform while minimizing forces in opposition. If one can effectively orchestrate this step of the process, the desired change will most likely occur. Force-field analysis allows one to determine the forces in favor and those opposed to change and to plan interventions that would mobilize the forces in favor of change and mitigate the forces opposing change.

Once change is made, a thorough evaluation of its effectiveness precedes the final step of institutionalizing the change, which ensures its continuation—even after the change agent is no longer present. In many ways, successfully affecting a transformational change necessitates the collective use of all of an administrator's knowledge and skills. It can be seen as the culminating activity of an educational leader.

IMPLICATIONS FOR PRACTICE: LEADERSHIP THROUGH TRANSITION CASE STUDY

Emergent is a college, turned comprehensive, turned regional research university. Currently, Emergent is striving to establish itself as a major national or tier-one research university. Emergent University sits near the US-Mexico border. It is a public university, and according to the Carnegie Classification, it is a research university with high activity. The research activities, as in many universities, are concentrated in particular pockets, like engineering and some social science areas.

University leaders have long nurtured what they call an "access and excellence" mission. Access has been provided through many means, such as the relatively open admissions policy. To this point, more than 95 percent of the students who apply are accepted, and the university has created many pathways for students to gain admission. The student body (22,000+) is 70 percent Latino identifying and is listed by the Hispanic Association of Colleges and Universities as a Hispanic-serving institution.

According to a presentation made by one of the university's top administrators, the vast majority of Emergent students work at least thirty hours per week. Very few graduate students go to school on graduate assistantships. Most graduate assistantship packages offer an annual salary of $12,000 to $14,000, and graduate students must still pay full tuition and fees.

Excellence, the other side of the equation, has been facilitated in a variety of ways. For Emergent, excellence is not defined as "selectivity in admissions" but in the fact that the organization innovatively works to provide students with many paths to access, with connections with their professors, and with validating relationships with the university in general.

However, around 2005, university leaders began to discuss the need to produce more research. For example, in university-wide speeches, the president and top administrators highlighted faculty who brought in research grants. Teaching and service were, of course, not ignored, but there was a heightened emphasis placed on research and grant attainment.

Around 2010, Emergent leaders began to press the need for transition particularly hard. The president gave interviews and testified at the state legislature about the viability of Emergent's research aspirations. University deans and chairs began to hold meetings with their faculties to discuss the changing expectations for tenure and promotion.

Administrators often discussed the idea that a national research reputation would translate into better experiences for their students. Off the record, administrators also shared that they were trying to remain competitive in a tight college admissions market, and they believed increasing their national ranking would increase applications and enrollment.

Whatever the reason for Emergent's striving, the transition is contingent on the work of organizational members, particularly the faculty. Most of the Emergent professors worried and wondered if the transition would undermine the student-centered culture or "friendliness" of the university, the open access mission, or the regional connectedness. In time, a majority of the faculty adopted a quiet resistance to Emergent's shifting mission.

When faculty were asked how they had or how they planned to change their work habits, they explained that they had little intention of making changes and would just carry on as they always had. In general, Emergent professors were concerned with teaching and ensured that their research grew directly out of their teaching experiences or student needs, if not the larger regional context, rather than taking direction from their disciplinary fields about what problems are the most important.

In general, the faculty was not moved by the dominant rules for earning prestige but preferred to serve their peers, their students, and the larger community in ways that upheld teaching and community connectedness. These professors, in other words, are not simply stubborn or resistant for the sake of being resistant; they are aiming to keep Emergent's original mission viable.

Over their years at Emergent, the professors crafted their teaching based on student interest and the regional culture of the area in which the university sits; many professors were attracted to Emergent for these very reasons. From their perspective, Emergent's top-tier, national research aspirations are likely to undercut the culture that they know so well.

Thus, these professors are working, or perhaps struggling, to preserve the mission and the work that they have built a career out of. They are struggling to prove that the careers that they have built still deserve a space inside their changing university. By responding with very little change, they are working quietly in hopes of securing such spaces.

As Emergent is now in its tenth year emphasizing the new, striving mission, administrators and faculty leaders have decided to assess whether or not the new research-oriented mission is improving the students' experiences, and a committee is now planning to develop and distribute an appropriate assessment to all students. In addition, a recent report from the Office of Admissions notes that Emergent has seen a 12 percent decline in application numbers and a 7 percent decline in enrollments.

DIAGNOSTIC DEBRIEF

Here are some questions that can be used to assess an institution's ability to change:

- Are all the steps of the integrated change model being implemented?
- Is a force-field analysis used during the change process?
- Are the intervention strategies appropriate for the situation?
- Do mechanisms exist for institutionalizing the change?

Chapter 11

Heart-Led Leadership

> Organization is not only directly linked to unity, but a natural development of that unity. Accordingly, the leaders' pursuit of that unity is also an attempt to organize the people, requiring witness to the fact the struggle for liberation is a common task.
>
> —*Paulo Freire*

Prior to this chapter, the focus of this book has been on knowledge and skill competency development. It is certainly helpful to become familiar with the theories that can be applied to a given workplace challenge. However, even with an arsenal of tools, leaders may still find themselves ineffective. How so? Because leading with the mind in the absence of the heart can actually present as an unattractive leadership trait.

How the leader utilizes the concepts contained in the preceding chapters of this book depends largely on their philosophy of life regarding how human beings behave in the workplace. The two extremes of the continuum might be described as those leaders who believe human beings are minimal performers and will do the very least they need to do to get by in the workplace and those who believe people are innately industrious and, if given the choice, would opt for doing a quality job.

It would seem the most effective leaders of modern times hold the latter view. Max De Pree, former owner and CEO of the highly successful Herman Miller Furniture Company, writes in his book *Leadership Is an Art* that a leader's function is to "liberate people to do what is required of them in the most effective and humane way possible" (De Pree, 1989). Instead of catching people doing something wrong, the goal as enlightened leaders is to catch them doing something right. It is suggested, therefore, in addition to a rational approach to leadership (leading with *mind*), a truly enlightened leader leads with heart.

Frequently, it seems, leaders underestimate the skills and qualities of their followers. Everyone is unique and harbors a distinctive skill set. What talents might a staff member possess that never get noticed or used in the organization? In any organization, there could be an Olympic athlete, book author, quilt maker, or chess master. People are multifaceted and, as such, so are the talents they can bring to the workplace.

Effectiveness of leadership begins with an understanding of the diversity of people's gifts, talents, and skills. When thinking about the variety of gifts people bring to organizations and institutions, one may come to see that leading with heart means cultivating, liberating, and enabling those gifts.

LEADERSHIP ENACTED

The first responsibility of a leader is to define reality through a vision. Their last responsibility is to say *thank you*. In the space between, leaders must become the servant of the servants. Being an educational leader means having the opportunity to make a meaningful difference in the lives of those who allow leaders to lead. To summarize, leaders who lead with heart do not inflict pain; they bear pain.

Whether one is a successful leader can be determined by looking at the followers. Are they reaching their potential? Are they learning? Are they able to change without bitterness? Are they able to achieve the institution's goals and objectives? Can they manage conflict among themselves? Leading with heart resides where the answers to these questions is an emphatic "Yes!"

Leadership can be considered in terms of one who serves to help and assist others. Fittingly, a leader owes something to the institution they lead. The leader is seen in this context as a steward rather than owner or proprietor. Leading with heart requires the leader to think about their stewardship in terms of legacy, direction, effectiveness, and values.

LEGACY

Regrettably, many leaders are singularly interested in immediate results that bolster their career goals. Long-range goals and planning are left to their successors. It is believed this approach fosters autocratic leadership, which often produces short-term results but militates against creativity and long-term benefits of innovative thinking. In effect, this approach is the antithesis of leading with heart.

On the contrary, leaders should build a long-lasting legacy of accomplishment that is institutionalized for posterity. They owe their institutions and their followers a healthy existence and the relationships and reputation that enable continuity of healthy existence. Leaders are also responsible for future leadership succession. They need to identify, develop, and nurture future leaders to carry on the legacy.

VALUES

Beyond succession planning, transformational leaders owe the individuals in their institution certain other legacies. Leaders need to be concerned with the institutional value system that determines the principles and standards guiding the practices of the organization. Leaders need to model their value systems so the individuals in the organization can learn to transmit these values to their colleagues and to future employees.

In a civilized institution, the visible display of good manners, respect for people, and an appreciation of the way in which people serve matters. A humane, sensitive, and thoughtful leader will transmit their value system through their daily behavior.

DIRECTION AND MOMENTUM

Through vision development, leaders oblige themselves to provide and maintain direction. As was previously discussed, effective leaders leave their organizations with a legacy. Part of this legacy should be a sense of progress or momentum, building a better tomorrow. An educational administrator, for instance, should imbue their institution with a sense of continuous progress, a sense of constant improvement.

Improvement and momentum come from a clear vision of what the institution ought to be, from a well-planned strategy to achieve that vision, and from carefully developed and articulated directions and plans that allow everyone to participate and feel personally accountable for achieving those plans.

SUPPORTING AND ENABLING

Supporting and enabling others to succeed is also a responsibility of leading with heart. Sanford (1967) coined the phrase "challenge and support," which means that optimal growth comes when challenges someone experiences are met with supports that can adequately tolerate the stress of the challenge itself. This practice calls for leaders to challenge followers to seek more, to work through challenging situations so participative decision-making and action-based learning can actualize.

Coinciding with *challenge*, the leader also provides adequate *support* so the follower is capable of successfully working through their challenge. Leaders need to enable others to reach their potential both personally and institutionally.

Leaders must realize that maximizing their own power and effectiveness requires empowering others. Leaders are responsible for setting and attaining the goals of their organizations. Empowering or enabling others to help achieve those goals enhances the leader's likelihood of success, ultimately enhancing the leader's effectiveness and power. Paradoxically, giving up power really amounts to gaining power.

TRUST AND RESPECT

Perspective is vital. Dwelling on the negative can lead to cynicism. Assuming an optimistic perspective, these are exciting times in education. Revolutionary steps are being taken to restructure educational systems and rethink the teaching-learning paradigm. The concepts of empowerment, total quality management, technology use, and strategic planning are becoming normal topics in educational conversations among leaders. Although these activities have the potential to influence education in significantly positive ways, they must be based on a strong foundation to achieve their full potential.

Achieving educational effectiveness is an incremental, sequential improvement process that begins by building a sense of security within each individual so they can be flexible in adapting to changes within their educational environment. Addressing only skills or techniques, such as communication, motivation, negotiation, or empowerment, is ineffective when individuals in an organization do not trust administration, policies, practices, and others in the workforce.

The challenge is to transform relationships based on insecurity, adversity, and politics to those based on a shared, mutual trust. Trust is the beginning of effectiveness and forms the foundation of a principle-centered learning environment that emphasizes strengths and devises innovative methods to minimize weaknesses. The transformation process requires an internal locus of control that emphasizes individual responsibility and accountability for change and for promoting effectiveness.

TEAMWORK

For many, there exists a dichotomy between how one sees themself as a person and how they see themself as a worker. Here, inspiration comes from a Zen Buddhist. They enlighten:

> The master in the art of living makes little distinction
> between his work and his play, his labor and his leisure,
> his mind and his body, his education and his recreation,
> his love and his religion. He hardly knows which is which.
> He simply pursues his vision of excellence in whatever he does,
> leaving others to decide whether he is working or playing.
> To him he is always doing both.

Productive, rewarding, enriching, fulfilling, and *joyful* are all words that should describe work. The ability to work is a great privilege, and it is up to leaders to make certain work is meaningful and fulfilling.

Paramount is the leadership ideal recognizing teamwork and the valuing of each individual's contribution to a final product. In essence, the synergy produced by an effective team is greater than the sum of its parts.

The foundation of the team is the recognition that each member needs every other member and no individual can be successful without the cooperation of others. Consider the story of a young boy who was a very enthusiastic baseball fan. The boy's favorite player was the Hall of Fame pitcher Robin Roberts of the Philadelphia Phillies.

During the early 1950s, Roberts's fastball dominated the National League. The boy's uncle, who took him to his first ballgame, explained that opposing batters were so intimidated by Roberts's fastball they were automatic "outs" even before they got to the plate. The uncle claimed Robin Roberts was unstoppable. But the young boy questioned this logic, for he knew no one was unstoppable. The boy retorted to his uncle that he knew how to stop Robin Roberts. "Make me his catcher!" he excitedly proclaimed. Success is lonely when it isn't shared.

OWNERSHIP EXPLORED

If an educational institution is to be successful, everyone in it needs to feel they are a part of its fabric. Taking ownership is a sign of one's love for an institution. In his book about servant leadership, Greenleaf (2008) posits, "Love is an indefinable term, and its manifestations are both subtle and infinite. It has only one absolute condition: unlimited liability!"

Although it might run counter to the traditional notion of American capitalism, employees should be encouraged to act as if they own the place. It is a sign of love (Greenleaf, 2008). Leaders have the responsibility to ensure all employees feel safe and encouraged to exercise this practice.

IMPLICATIONS FOR PRACTICE: HEART-LED LEADERSHIP CASE STUDY

Dr. Thomas Lead, the president of Hopeful University, a private liberal arts institution with a growing graduate studies program, recently received a resolution from the faculty senate. In the resolution, the faculty unanimously threatened a vote of no confidence if Dr. Lead did not "address spiraling athletics department costs and overhead" and "realign the priorities of the institution to its mission of academic excellence in the liberal arts."

Dr. Lead acknowledges there has been a push to enhance Hopeful's athletics programs, especially in light of the name recognition and branding possibilities of a winning national program, as well as data indicating Hopeful's student-athletes maintain some of the highest GPAs on campus. In fact, enhancing the athletics program is a part of Hopeful's five-year strategic plan and is a marketed objective in a major capital campaign.

Yet, due to the economic recession and the rising overhead costs of athletic facilities, salaries, and scholarships, the institution's budget has been hit hard, and Dr. Lead made the difficult decision to reduce faculty professional development funding and modestly cut the budget of the Office of Student Life in order to maintain supports for athletics.

Concerned about the faculty senate's growing discontent, Dr. Lead sets up a meeting with Dr. Lisa Ahern, the recently appointed director of planning for Hopeful University, to craft a response to the faculty senate. He wishes to do right by all employees of the university, faculty, staff, and administration. How should Dr. Lead respond to faculty senate concerns?

DIAGNOSTIC DEBRIEF

Here are some questions that can be used to assess a leader's ability to lead with heart:

- Is there is a tendency to merely go through the motions?
- Is finding time to celebrate accomplishments problematic or encouraged?
- Do employees harness cynicism or optimism when faced with challenges?
- Is leadership merely accumulating power or sharing it?

- Are grace, style, and civility leading practices when engaging with others?
- Do administrators dwell on individuals' weaknesses or their strengths?
- Are diversity and individual charisma respected?

Chapter 12

Engaging the Material

> So often in life things that you regard as an impediment turn out to be great good fortune.
>
> —*Ruth Bader Ginsburg*

It is time to bring this book to a close. What has been learned about organizational development and leadership in the last eleven chapters of this text? First, readers learned a systematic way of diagnosing an institution's organizational health—namely, by constantly assessing the eleven components of an organization. Second, readers gained the knowledge and skills to address many weaknesses found in school organizations and leadership in general.

Situational or contingency leadership theory as a solid grounded approach was also discovered. Contemporary trailblazers and aspiring leaders need to adapt their leadership behavior to changing situations. The truly heroic leaders are successful because they are able to very effectively balance multiple challenges while maintaining a strong moral frame and appreciation for all humanity. Finally, readers learned the importance of organizational development and leadership *theory*.

THE IMPORTANCE OF THEORY

The importance of theory should not be underestimated. Theory is valuable. Its importance in the field of organizational development and leadership can be illustrated through proper diagnosis, analysis, and correction of failed practice. Without a theoretical base, one is left to risk leading by trial and error.

Theory is to leadership as the fundamentals of sound making is to speech development. For example, an infant will find learning the art of language considerably more difficult if they are not exposed to making sounds, enunciation, and sound patterns. Throughout the learning process, it is likely one or more of these fundamentals will be forgotten and cause a lapse in development. However, when corrected, speech development will rise again.

In the absence of dedicated time and effort, a child can still develop speech through the very inefficient means of trial and error. The same goes for leaders who are losing their impact on their followers. If they have not adopted a leadership theory to guide their behavior, they can only correct the leadership decline by trial and error.

However, if the leader has internalized a leadership theory, the leader can review the tenets or principles of the theory and most likely diagnose the deficiency and correct it rather quickly. For example, the leader might find their followers are no longer responding to the leader's friendly persuasion and active support (human resource leadership behavior).

In analyzing the situation, the leader might conclude they are using human resource behavior with followers when structural leadership behavior may be more appropriate. As a result of this analysis, the leader may decide to utilize a more structural approach with their recalcitrant followers. This rather simple example demonstrates the importance and value of theory in providing leaders with the knowledge and skills they need to diagnose and correct failed practice in an efficient and effective way.

MINDFULNESS IN LEADERSHIP

Knowledge is a prerequisite for effective leadership. Competency usually manifests itself in one's structural frame of leadership. In sports terms, the leader must have a good command of the fundamentals of the game. In business terms, the effective leader must have a thorough knowledge of the technical aspects of how a business operates and a sense of how to develop a viable business plan.

In education, the transformational leader needs to know how educational systems operate and best practices in curriculum, instruction, and assessment. In a family situation, the leader (parent, guardian, or caregiver) needs to have at least a modicum of knowledge regarding the principles of child psychology. In short, leaders in any field require knowledge to act effectively. Praxis is then actualized when one applies knowledge through theory and practice. In this book the following organizational development topics were discussed:

- Organizational structure: how an institution is organized
- Organizational culture: the values and beliefs of an institution
- Leadership theories and models: how leadership is developed
- Mindset and motivation: growth mindset and systems of rewards and incentives

- Decision-making: how and by whom decisions are made
- Communication: the clarity and accuracy of the communication process
- Conflict management: how dysfunctional conflict is handled
- Power distribution: how the power in an institution is distributed
- Strategic planning: how the mission, vision, and strategic plan are developed
- Leadership through change: how change is effectively implemented in an institution
- Heart-led leadership: whether a culture of trust and respect prevails in an institution

Included in the appendix is a pair of diagnostic tools entitled The Heart Smart Survey I and II, which the authors developed to help leaders assess the organizational health of their institutions. Heart Smart I assesses whether the leaders are leading with *mind*, and Heart Smart II assesses whether the leaders are leading with *heart*. Together they identify which of the factors listed above need improvement.

HEART-LED LEADERSHIP

To review, an effective leader needs competency. However, only being smart is ill-advised. To be truly effective and heroic, leaders need to master the *art* of leadership and learn to lead with *heart*. In effect, leaders need to operate out of both the structural and political frames (science) and the human resources, symbolic, and moral frames (art) to maximize their effectiveness. Leaders must be concerned about all aspects of a person: mental, emotional, physical, and spiritual. *Cura personalis* is a Latin phrase capturing the essence of caring for the whole person.

While not explicitly discussed in chapter 11, leaders must abide by the Golden Rule and treat others as they wish to be treated. As noted earlier, truly effective leaders respect their employees as much as they respect volunteers. Leaders empower their workforce to actualize true potential within each person, thus engendering mutual trust and respect among their colleagues.

In their book entitled *Leading with Kindness* (2008), William Baker and Michael O'Malley reiterate the views expressed in this book. They explore how one of the most unheralded features of leadership, basic human kindness, drives successful organizations. And while most scholars generally recognize that a leader's emotional intelligence factors into their leadership behavior, most are reluctant to consider it to be as important as analytical ability, decision-making skills, or implementation skills.

Such emotions as compassion, empathy, and kindness are often dismissed as unquantifiable and are often seen as weaknesses. Yet, research in neuroscience and the social sciences reveals one's physiological and emotional states have measurable effects on both individual and group performance.

A high level of emotional intelligence is inculcated in individuals who lead with heart or kindness. Many are familiar with the current notion of multiple intelligences; that is, individuals have a number of intelligences in addition to cognitive intelligence. Among these intelligences is emotional intelligence. Several theories within the emotional intelligence paradigm seek to understand how individuals perceive, understand, utilize, and manage emotions in an effort to predict and foster personal effectiveness.

Most of these models define emotional intelligence as an array of traits and abilities related to emotional and social knowledge that influence an overall ability to effectively cope with environmental demands; as such, it can be viewed as a model of psychological well-being and adaptation. This includes the ability to be aware of, to understand, and to relate to others; the ability to deal with strong emotions and to control one's impulses; and the ability to adapt to change and to solve problems of a personal and social nature.

Emotional intelligence models have five domains: intrapersonal skills, interpersonal skills, adaptability, stress management, and general mood. If the reader sees a similarity between emotional intelligence and what is being termed *heart-led leadership* and what Baker and O'Malley (2008) call *leading with kindness*, it is not coincidental.

LEADING WITH MIND AND HEART

Truly heroic leaders utilize *both* mind (science) and heart (art)—with cognitive intelligence and emotional intelligence. One without the other will not suffice. Only by mastering both will the leader succeed.

For example, former president Donald Trump was rendered ineffective as a leader because of his tenacious push to share inaccurate and unsubstantiated claims of widespread voter fraud, which led to the January 2021 insurrection on Capitol Hill by Trump supporters. Why was he deemed ineffective? Because he suddenly lost the *knowledge* of how government works (science)? No! He lost his ability to lead because he lost the *trust and respect* of much of the American public (art). He could still lead with his mind, but he had lost the ability to lead with heart. It remains to be determined how long it will take for him to reestablish his integrity with the American public.

On the contrary, one could argue that former president Jimmy Carter lost his ability to lead because of a perceived lack of competency. The majority of the voting public did not believe he had the knowledge necessary to manage government operations and effectively lead with mind. However, President Carter's concern for people, his integrity, and his ability to lead with heart was virtually unquestioned. Absent the perceived ability to do *both*, however, he lost the 1980 election to Ronald Reagan.

We conclude, then, that effective leaders are situational; that is, they are capable of adapting their leadership behavior to the situation. They utilize structural, human resources, symbolic, political, and moral leadership behavior when appropriate. They lead with both mind (structural and political behavior) and with heart (human resources, symbolic, and moral behavior). They master both the science (mind) and art (heart) of leadership, and, in doing so, they are transformational, leading their organizations to new heights. As Chris Lowney (2003) writes in *Heroic Leadership*, such leaders are, in a word, truly "heroic."

CONCLUSION

The intention of this textbook is to provide a rich overview of the attributes and functional areas needed for true leadership formation. To this end, the authors have attempted to create a go-to guide for aligning mind and heart in leadership and organizational dynamics.

Each chapter presents key components to ensure success for educational leaders as they strive to be effective agents of change. Together, the topics offered herein provide foundational theory to support practice in the field. These components work in tandem to ensure effective educational organization management.

Appendix: Heart Smart Surveys I and II

(FROM *ALIGNING MIND AND HEART*, HEASLEY & PALESTINI, 2022)

Similar to processes by which individual health is measured, there are ways to assess the health of an educational institution or departments and units within. Heart Smart Survey I may be used to identify vital signs in an organization or org system. This survey and its complement, Heart Smart Survey II, can help determine whether institutional leaders are directing from both mind and heart.

HEART SMART SURVEY I

When taking this survey, the participant should think of their present work environment and indicate their level of agreement (1 = *strongly disagree*, 7 = *strongly agree*) with each of the following statements.

Strongly Disagree	Disagree	Slightly Disagree	Neither Disagree nor Agree	Slightly Agree	Agree	Strongly Agree
1	2	3	4	5	6	7

1. The tasks in this institution are divided in a logical way.
2. The relationships among coworkers are harmonious.
3. The institution's leadership efforts result in the fulfillment of its purposes.
4. My work at this institution offers me an opportunity to grow as a person.
5. I can always talk to someone at work if I have a work-related problem.

6. Employees (staff and faculty) actively participate in decisions.
7. There is little evidence of unresolved conflict in this institution.
8. There is a strong fit between this institution's mission and my own values.
9. The faculty and staff are represented on most committees and task forces.
10. Professional development routinely accompanies any significant changes that occur in this institution.
11. The tasks in this institution are distributed fairly.
12. The opinions of employees are valued, regardless of one's length of tenure or employment in the organization.
13. The administrators display the behaviors required for effective leadership.
14. The rewards and incentives here are both internal and external.
15. There is open and direct communication among all levels of this institution.
16. Participative decision-making is fostered at this institution.
17. What little conflict exists at this institution is not dysfunctional.
18. Representatives of all segments of the school community participate in the strategic planning process.
19. All employees (faculty and staff) have an appropriate voice in the operation of this institution.
20. This institution is not resistant to constructive change.
21. The division of labor in this organization helps in its efforts to reach its goals.
22. I feel valued by this institution.
23. The administration encourages an appropriate amount of participation in decision-making.
24. Faculty and staff members are often recognized for special achievements.
25. There are no significant barriers to effective communication at this institution.
26. When the acceptance of a decision is important, a group decision-making model is used.
27. There are mechanisms at this institution to effectively manage conflict and stress.
28. Most of the employees understand the mission and goals of this institution.
29. The faculty and staff feel empowered to make their own decisions regarding their daily work.
30. Tolerance toward change is modeled by the administration of this institution.
31. The various grade-level teachers and departments work well together.
32. Differences among people are accepted.

33. The leadership is able to generate continuous improvement in the institution.
34. My ideas are encouraged, recognized, and used.
35. Communication is carried out in a nonaggressive style.
36. In general, the decision-making process is effective.
37. Conflicts are usually resolved before they become dysfunctional.
38. For the most part, the employees of this institution feel an ownership of its goals.
39. The faculty and staff are encouraged to be creative in their work.
40. Changes are made within a rational process.
41. This institution's organizational design responds well to changes in the internal and external environment.
42. The teaching and non-teaching staffs get along with one another.
43. The leadership of this institution espouses a clear educational vision.
44. The goals and objectives for the year are mutually developed by the faculty, staff, and administration.
45. I believe my opinions and ideas are listened to.
46. Usually, a collaborative style of decision-making is utilized at this institution.
47. A collaborative approach to conflict resolution is ordinarily used.
48. This institution has a clear educational vision.
49. The faculty and staff can express their opinions without fear of retribution.
50. I feel confident that I will have an opportunity for input if a significant change were to take place in this institution.
51. This institution is people oriented.
52. Administrators, staff, and faculty show each other mutual respect.
53. Administrators and supervisors give people the freedom to do their job.
54. The rewards and incentives in this institution are designed to satisfy a variety of individual needs.
55. The opportunity for feedback is always available in the communications process.
56. Group decision-making techniques, like brainstorming and group surveys, are sometimes used in the decision-making process.
57. Conflicts are often prevented by early intervention.
58. This institution has a strategic plan for the future.
59. Most administrators here use the power of persuasion rather than the power of coercion.
60. This institution is committed to continually improving through the process of change.
61. This institution does not adhere to a strict chain of command.
62. This institution exhibits grace, style, and civility.

63. The administrators model desired behavior.
64. At this institution, employees are not normally coerced into doing things.
65. I have the information I need to do a good job.
66. I can constructively challenge the decisions in this institution.
67. A process to resolve work-related grievances is available.
68. There is an ongoing planning process at this institution.
69. The faculty and staff have input into the operation of this institution through a collective bargaining unit or through a shared governance body, system, or practice.
70. The policies, procedures, and programs of this institution are periodically reviewed.

Instructions: Transfer the numerical value from the response scale on the questionnaire to the blanks below. Add each column, and divide each sum by 7. This will give comparable scores for each of the ten areas.

S	C	L	M	CO	D	CR	G	P	A
1.___	2.___	3.___	4.___	5.___	6.___	7.___	8.___	9.___	10.___
11.___	12.___	13.___	14.___	15.___	16.___	17.___	18.___	19.___	20.___
21.___	22.___	23.___	24.___	25.___	26.___	27.___	28.___	29.___	30.___
31.___	32.___	33.___	34.___	35.___	36.___	37.___	38.___	39.___	40.___
41.___	42.___	43.___	44.___	45.___	46.___	47.___	48.___	49.___	50.___
51.___	52.___	53.___	54.___	55.___	56.___	57.___	58.___	59.___	60.___
61.___	62.___	63.___	64.___	65.___	66.___	67.___	68.___	69.___	70.___

Total

Average

Score Card Legend

S = Structure, C = Culture, L = Leadership, M = Motivation, CO = Communication, D = Decision-Making, CR = Conflict Resolution, G = Goal Setting/Planning, P = Power Distribution, A = Attitude Toward Change

Interpretation Sheet

Once the participant has transferred scores for each question, they will calculate the average score for each column and write it in the appropriately labeled row on the scoring sheet. Background information and interpretation suggestions are provided below.

Background

The Heart Smart Organizational Diagnosis Questionnaire is a survey-feedback instrument designed to collect data on organizational functioning. It measures the perceptions of persons in an organization to determine areas of activity that would benefit from an organizational development effort. It can be used as the sole data-collection technique or in conjunction with other techniques (interview, observation, etc.). The instrument and the model reflect a systematic approach for analyzing relationships among variables that influence how an organization is managed. Using the Heart Smart Organizational Diagnosis Questionnaire is the first step in determining appropriate interventions for organizational change efforts.

Interpretation and Diagnosis

It is crucial that diagnosis be based on data interpretation. The simplest diagnosis is to assess the amount of variance for each of the ten variables in relation to a score of 4, which is the neutral point. Scores below 4 indicate a problem with organizational functioning. The closer the score is to 1, the more severe the problem. Scores above 4 indicate the lack of a problem, with a score of 7 indicating optimum functioning.

Another diagnostic approach follows the same guidelines of assessment in relation to the neutral point (score) of 4. The score of each of the seventy items on the questionnaire can be reviewed to produce more exacting information on problematic areas. Thus, diagnosis would be more precise. For example, suppose that the average score on item number 8 is 1.4. This would indicate not only a problem in organizational purpose or goal setting but also a more specific problem in that there is a gap between organizational and individual goals. This more precise diagnostic effort is likely to lead to a more appropriate intervention in the organization than the generalized diagnostic approach described in the preceding paragraph.

Appropriate diagnosis must address the relationships between the boxes to determine the interconnectedness of problems. For example, if there is a problem with communication, could it be that the organizational structure does not foster effective communication? This might be the case if the average score on item 25 was well below 4 (2.5 or lower) and all the items on organizational structure (1, 11, 21, 31, 41, 51, 61) also averaged below 4.0.

HEART SMART SURVEY II

Participants of this survey should center their thoughts on their present work environment and indicate their level of agreement (1 = *strongly agree*, 7 = *strongly disagree*) with each of the following statements.

Strongly Agree	Agree	Slightly Agree	Neither Disagree nor Agree	Slightly Disagree	Disagree	Strongly Disagree
1	2	3	4	5	6	7

1. There is not much evidence of faculty and staff holding and espousing ethical values.
2. There is not much evidence of mutual respect and understanding among all employees.
3. There is not much of a sense of voluntarism and dedication among the faculty and staff.
4. There is not much indication that employees (administration, faculty, and staff) have committed themselves to the modeling of moral and ethical values.
5. There is not much trust and respect shared among faculty, staff, and administration.
6. There is little evidence that faculty encourage students to be concerned for the underserved in their communities.
7. There is not much evidence that the faculty are supportive of a moral or ethical code to guide one's behavior.
8. There are not many occasions when the administration, faculty, and staff get to interact with one another.
9. There are not many opportunities presented to students to develop an appreciation of and respect for cultures other than their own.
10. Faculty do not often bear witness to their values and beliefs through their daily behavior.
11. The administration, faculty, and staff do not seem to support one another in various events and activities.
12. There are not many occasions when faculty members accompany their students on community service activities.
13. There are no occasions when faculty and students discuss their values and beliefs.
14. There is not much in the way of promotion of justice and fairness among students.
15. There is not a culture that fosters service to the community at this institution.

16. The faculty does not seem to go out of its way to model their belief system to the students.
17. There is not much evidence of the promotion of justice and fairness among employees.
18. There are not many occasions when employees engage in community service by donating space, time, resources, and personal help.
19. There are not many times when the administration, faculty, and staff articulate or speak out on their values and beliefs.
20. There is not much evidence of the promotion of justice and fairness between faculty and administrators.
21. There are not many instances of faculty evidencing compassion and giving service to the needy, the disadvantaged, and troubled students and coworkers.
22. There are not many occasions when the faculty discusses teaching values and ethics.
23. There are significant barriers to effective communication at this institution.
24. The overall morale of the school is not very good.
25. The faculty and staff do not show much concern for world problems like hunger, poverty, war, pollution, and social justice.
26. The faculty does not openly express its support of ethical and moral values.
27. The conflicts that arise among individuals and groups are not resolved very well.
28. The faculty and staff do not encourage a sense of service and social justice in their students very much.
29. The faculty do not avail themselves of professional development opportunities to develop their skills in teaching values education.
30. The sense of trust and respect at this institution is not very high.
31. There is a tendency to merely go through the motions within this organization.
32. There is a tendency for the superficial to be more important than the substantial at this institution.
33. There is a dark tension that exists among key individuals at this school.
34. It seems that the attainment of short-term goals is preferred to the achievement of long-term goals.
35. There seems to be a loss of grace, style, and civility at this institution.
36. There is a tendency to do the minimal and not go the extra yard at this school.
37. The administration seems to use coercion to motivate employees here.
38. We do not ever seem to be able to find the time to celebrate accomplishments here.

39. The administration, faculty, and staff seem to treat students like customers or impositions.
40. The employees feel manipulated and exploited here.
41. There don't seem to be many stories and storytellers to carry on the tradition at this school.
42. The leaders here seem to want to be served rather than to serve.
43. There seems to be a certain arrogance among the leaders at this school.
44. There seems to be a sense of competition here whereby one person or group's gain always has to be at another's expense.
45. Administration and faculty would never pick up a piece of paper because "that's the janitor's job."
46. When something goes wrong here, there is a tendency to want to cast blame.
47. Diversity and individual charisma are not respected here.
48. Employees seem to use up all their sick days even if they are not sick.
49. The administration seems to accumulate power rather than sharing it at this institution.
50. The climate in this school seems to encourage competition rather than collaboration.
51. Employees seem to work solely for a paycheck here.
52. Faculty are asked to prioritize and track proficiency and achievement toward student learning rather than individual student growth toward this goal.
53. There is a tendency for the faculty rooms to be sources of malicious gossip and rumors.
54. There is a union mentality here whereby workers do not want to do anything extra unless they are paid.
55. Administrators here seem to dwell on people's weaknesses rather than their strengths.
56. Individual turf and claim to space is protected to the detriment of institutional goals at this institution.
57. There exists a definite caste system among the administration, faculty, and the clerical and custodian staffs.

Instructions: Transfer the numerical value from the response scale on the questionnaire to the blanks below. Add each column, and divide each sum by 19. This will give you comparable scores for each of the three areas measured by this instrument.

Moral Integrity	Community	Service/Social Justice
1.___	2.___	3.___
4.___	5.___	6.___
7.___	8.___	9.___
10.___	11.___	12.___
13.___	14.___	15.___
16.___	17.___	18.___
19.___	20.___	21.___
22.___	23.___	24.___
25.___	26.___	27.___
28.___	29.___	30.___
31.___	32.___	33.___
34.___	35.___	36.___
37.___	38.___	39.___
40.___	41.___	42.___
43.___	44.___	45.___

Moral Integrity	Community	Service/Social Justice
46.___	47.___	48.___
49.___	50.___	51.___
52.___	53.___	54.___
55.___	56.___	57.___

Total

Average
(sum score divided by 19)

Interpretation Sheet

The information that follows provides background information and interpretation suggestions for Heart Smart Survey II.

Background

Heart Smart Organizational Diagnosis Questionnaires are survey-feedback instruments designed to collect data on organizational functioning. They measure the perceptions of persons in an organization to determine areas of activity that would benefit from an organizational development effort. It can be used as the sole data-collection technique or in conjunction with other techniques (interview, observation, etc.). The instrument and the model reflect a systematic approach for analyzing relationships among variables that influence how an organization is managed. Using the Heart Smart Organizational Diagnosis Questionnaires is the first step in determining appropriate interventions for organizational change efforts.

Interpretation and Diagnosis

It is crucial that diagnosis be based on data interpretation. The simplest diagnosis is to assess the amount of variance for each of the three variables in relation to a score of 4, which is the neutral point. Scores below 4 indicate a problem with organizational functioning. The closer the score is to 1, the more severe the problem. Scores above 4 indicate the lack of a problem, with a score of 7 indicating optimum functioning.

Another diagnostic approach follows the same guidelines of assessment in relation to the neutral point (score) of 4. The score of each of the fifty-seven items on the questionnaire can be reviewed to produce more exacting information on problematic areas. Thus, diagnosis would be more precise. For example, let us suppose that the average score on item number 8 is 2.3. This indicates not only a problem in the sense of community in the institution but also a more specific problem in that there are not enough occasions provided for the employees to interact with one another. This more precise diagnostic effort is likely to lead to a more appropriate intervention in the organization than the generalized diagnostic approach described in the preceding paragraph.

HEART SMART ORGANIZATION DIAGNOSIS QUESTIONNAIRES

Just as there are vital signs in measuring individual health, the authors of these instruments believe there are ways to accurately assess the health of institutions. These surveys may help identify important vital signs in the institution or a department or unit within the system. The purpose of the Heart Smart Organizational Diagnosis Questionnaires, therefore, is to provide feedback data for intensive diagnostic efforts. Use of the questionnaires, either by themselves or in conjunction with other information-collecting techniques, such as systematic observation, individual interviews, or focus groups, may very well provide the data needed to identify strengths and weaknesses in the functioning of an educational institution and help determine whether employees are leading with both mind and heart.

A meaningful diagnostic effort must be based on a theory or model of organizational development. This makes action research possible as it facilitates problem identification, which is essential to determining the proper functioning of an organization. The model suggested here establishes a systematic approach for analyzing relationships among the variables that influence how an organization is managed. Heart Smart Survey I provides for assessment in ten areas of formal and informal activity (see Heart Smart Wheel Diagram).

Heart Smart Survey II provides for assessment of three areas of formal and informal activity: moral integrity, a sense of community, and a dedication to service and social justice.

The outer periphery in the following diagram represents an organizational boundary for diagnosis. This boundary demarcates the functioning of the internal and external environments. Since the underlying organizational theory on which this survey is based is an open systems model, it is essential that influences from both the internal and external environment be considered for the analysis to be complete.

THE HEART SMART WHEEL DIAGRAM STRUCTURE

How is this institution organized?

Conflict Resolution	*Culture*
Is the institution functional or dysfunctional?	What values and beliefs are important here?
Goal Setting and Planning	**Leadership**
Are the goals clear, accepted, and operationalized?	How effectively are the boxes kept in balance?
INTERNAL	*ENVIRONMENT*
Power Distribution	**Motivation**
Are the faculty and staff empowered?	Are the rewards and incentives effective?
Attitude	**Communication**
Is the institution continually improving?	Is the message being transmitted clearly?
Decision-Making	
How and by whom are decisions being made?	
Internal Environment	**External Environment**

References

Adams, J. L. (1986). *The care and feeding of ideas: A guide to encouraging creativity*. Reading, MA: Addison-Wesley.

Alagaraja, M., & Herd, A. M. (2022). Understanding multi-level learning in organizations: A comparison of lean and the learning organization. *Performance Improvement Quarterly, 34*(4), 521–546.

Anderson, M. (2017). Transformational leadership in education: A review of existing literature. *International Social Science Review, 93*(1), 1–13.

Ärlestig, H. (2008). In school communication: Developing a pedagogically focused school culture. *Values and Ethics in Educational Administration, 7*(1).

Arneson, S. (2015). Improving teaching, one conversation at a time. *Educational Leadership, 72*(7), 32–36.

Bailey, M. R., Simpson, E. H., & Balsam, P. D. (2018). Neural substrates underlying effort, time, and risk-based decision making in motivated behavior. *Neurobiology of Learning and Memory, 133*, 233–256.

Baker, W., & O'Malley, M. (2008). *Leading with kindness*. New York: AMACOM.

Balch, T., Oliver, B., Phelps, C., & Balch, B. (2021). *Building great mental health professional-teacher teams: A systematic approach to social-emotional learning for students and educators*. Bloomington, IN: Solution Tree Press.

Bandura, A. (1978). *Social learning theory*. Englewood Cliffs, NJ: Prentice Hall.

Blanchard, K., & Johnson, S. (1982). *One-minute manager*. New York: William Morrow & Company.

Bolman, L. G., & Deal, T. E. (1991). *Reframing organizations: Artistry, choice, and leadership*. San Francisco: Jossey-Bass.

Bryson, J. M. (2018). *Strategic planning for public and nonprofit organizations: A guide to strengthening and sustaining organizational achievement*, 5th ed. Hoboken, NJ: Wiley.

Carlson, R. (1990). Conscious mental episodes and skill acquisition. *Behavioral and Brain Sciences, 13*, 599.

Chapple, C. (1993). *The Jesuit tradition in education and missions*. Scranton, NY: University of Scranton Press.

Chen, Li F., & Leung, K. (2016). When does supervisor support encourage innovative behavior? Opposite moderating effects of general self-efficacy and internal locus of control. *Personnel Psychology, 69*(1), 123–158.

Delmestri, G., & Goodrick, E. (2016). Looking away: Denial and emotions in institutional stability and change. *How Institutions Matter, 48A,* 233–271.

Deming, W. E. (2000). *Out of crisis.* Boston: MIT Press.

De Pree, M. (1989). *Leadership is an art.* New York: Dell.

Drew, C. (2020). *8 models of communication explained.* Retrieved from https://helpfulprofessor.com/communication-models/.

Dufresne, R. L., Botto, K., & Steele, E. S. (2015). Contributing to an Ignatian perspective on leadership. *Journal of Jesuit Business Education, 6,* 1–19.

Dweck, C. (2008). *Mindset: The new psychology of success.* New York: Ballantine Books.

Engle, M., & Gonzalez, J. V. (2014). Leading and teaching with cultural competence. *Leadership, 44*(2), 34–36.

Flostrand, A., Pitt, L., & Bridson, S. (2020). The Delphi technique in forecasting—A 42-year bibliographic analysis (1975–2017). *Technological Forecasting & Social Change, 150,* https://doi.org/10.1016/j.techfore.2019.119773.

Glasser, W. (1984). *Control theory, a new explanation of how we control our lives.* New York: Harper & Row.

Goncalves, M. (2012). *Learning organizations: Turning knowledge into actions.* New York: Business Expert Press.

Gordon, J. R. (1993). *A diagnostic approach to organizational behavior.* Boston: Allyn & Bacon.

Greenleaf, R. K. (2008). *The servant as leader.* Terre Haute, IN: Greenleaf Center for Servant Leadership.

Hanson, E. M. (1991). *Educational administration and organizational behavior.* Boston: Allyn & Bacon.

Hart, A. W. (1987). A career ladder's effect on teacher career and work attitudes. *American Educational Research Journal, 24*(4), 479–503.

Heasley, C., & Palestini, R. (2022). *Aligning mind and heart: Leadership and organization dynamics for advancing K-12 education.* New York: Rowman & Littlefield Publishers.

Heilman, M. E., & Stopeck, M. H. (1985). Being attractive, advantage or disadvantage? Performance evaluations and recommended personnel actions as a function of appearance, sex, and job type. *Organizational Behavior and Human Decision Processes, 35,* 202–215.

Hersey, P., & Blanchard, K. H. (1979). Life-cycle theory of leadership. *Training and Development Journal, 23,* 26–34.

Hersey, P., & Blanchard, K. H. (1988). *Management of organizational behavior,* 5th ed. Englewood Cliffs, NJ: Prentice Hall.

Hersey, P., & Blanchard, K. H. (1996). Great ideas revisited: Life-cycle theory of leadership. *Training & Development, 50*(1), 42–53.

Jones, T. M. (1991). Ethical decision-making by individuals in organizations: An issue-contingent model. *Academy of Management Review, 16*(2), 366–395.

Kaplan, A. (1964). *Power in perspective, in power and conflict in organizations*, ed. R. L. Kahn and E. Boulding. London: Tavistock.

Kirkpatrick, S. A., & Locke, E. A. (1991). Leadership: Do traits matter? *Academy of Management Executive*, 5(2), 49.

Kotter, J. P. (1977). Power, dependence, and effective management. *Harvard Business Review*, 55, 125–136.

Kotter, J. P. (1978). Power, success, and organizational effectiveness. *Organizational Dynamics*, 6, 27–40.

Lewin, K. (1951). *Field theory in social science*. London, UK: Tavistock Publications.

Lewis, P. V. (1987). *Organizational communication: The essence of effective management*, 3rd ed. New York: Wiley.

Lowney, C. (2003). *Heroic leadership*. Chicago: Loyola Press.

Loyola, I. (2007). *The spiritual exercises of St. Ignatius of Loyola*. New York: Cosimo Classics.

Lührs, N., et al. (2018). How participatory should environmental governance be? Testing the applicability of the Vroom-Yetton-Jago Model in public environmental decision-making. *Environmental Management (New York)*, 61(2), 249–262.

Maslow, A. H. (1987). *Motivation and personality*, 3rd ed. New York: Harper & Row.

Meier, D. (2016). Situational leadership theory as a foundation for a blended learning framework. *Journal of Education and Practice*, 7(10), 25–30.

Michaelsen, L. K., Watson, W. E., and Black, R. H. (1989). A realistic test of individual vs. group consensus decision-making. *Journal of Applied Psychology*, 74(5), 834–839.

Murphy, J. (1988). Methodological, measurement, and conceptual problems in the study of instructional leadership. *Educational Evaluation and Policy Analysis*, 10(1), 117.

National Association of Elementary School Principals (2008). *Leading learning communities: Standards for what principals should know and be able to do*, 2nd ed. Collaborative Communications Group.

Neubert, M. J., & Dyck, B. (2016). Developing sustainable management theory: Goal-setting theory based in virtue. *Management Decision*, 54(2), 304–320.

Oliver, S., & Duncan, S. (2019). Editorial: Looking through the Johari window. *Research for All*, 3(1), 1–6.

Palestini, R. (2000). *Ten steps to educational reform: Making change happen*. Lanham, MD: Rowman & Littlefield Education.

Palestini, R. (2011). *Educational administration: Leading with mind and heart*, 3rd ed. Lanham, MD: Rowman & Littlefield Education.

Palestini, R. (2013). *No laughing matter: The value of humor in educational leadership*. Lanham, MD: Rowman & Littlefield Education.

Pavlov, I. (1927). *Conditioned reflexes: An investigation of the physiological activity of the cerebral cortex*. Trans. and ed. G. V. Anrep. London: Oxford University Press.

Peters, T., & Waterman, R. (1988). *In search of excellence*. New York: Grand Central.

Pfajfar, G., et al. (2019). Power source drivers and performance outcomes of functional and dysfunctional conflict in exporter–importer relationships. *Industrial*

Marketing Management, 78, 213–226. https://doi.org/10.1016/j.indmarman.2017.03.005.

Polevoi, L. (2012). Effective communication starts with you. *Managing People at Work*, (362), 5.

Rahim, M. A. (1989). Relationships of leader power to compliance and satisfaction with supervision: Evidence from a national sample of managers. *Journal of Management, 15*(4), 545–556.

Rest, J. R. (1986). *Moral development: Advances in research and theory*. New York: Praeger.

Rowe, G., & Wright, G. (1999). The Delphi technique as a forecasting tool: Issues and analysis. *International Journal of Forecasting, 15*(4), 353–375, https://doi.org/10.1016/S0169-2070(99)00018-7.

Sanaghan, P. (2009). *Collaborative strategic planning in higher education*. Washington, DC: NACUBO.

Sanford, N. (1967). The development of social responsibility. *American Journal of Orthopsychiatry, 37*(1), 22–29. https://doi.org/10.1111/j.1939-0025.1967.tb01063.x.

Seaton, F. S. (2018). Empowering teachers to implement a growth mindset. *Educational Psychology in Practice, 34*(1), 41–57.

Senge, P. M. (1990). *The fifth dimension: The art of practice of the learning organization*. New York: Doubleday.

Simon, H. A. (1960). *The new science of management decision*. New York: Harper.

Stout, J. G., & Dasgupta, N. (2013). Mastering one's destiny: Mastery goals promote challenge and success despite social identity threat. *Personality & Social Psychology Bulletin, 39*(6), 748–762.

Team Leverage Edu. (2020). *Modes of communication*. Retrieved from: https://leverageedu.com/blog/modes-of-communication/.

Thomas, J. B., McDaniel, Jr., R. R., and Dooris, M. J. (1989). Strategic issue analysis: NGT + decision analysis for resolving strategic issues, *Journal of Applied Behavioral Sciences, 25*(2), 189–200, for more recent examples.

Thorndike, E. L. (1924). *Behaviorism*. New York: Norton.

Tolman, E. C. (1932). *Purposive behavior in animals and men*. New York: Appleton-Century-Crofts.

Tripole, M. R., SJ. (1994). *Faith beyond justice*. St. Louis, MO: Institute of Jesuit Sources.

Vance, R., & Colella, A. (1990). Effects of two types of feedback on goal acceptance and personal goals. *Journal of Applied Psychology, 75*, 68–76.

Vroom, V. H. and Jago, E. J. (1988). *The New Leadership: Managing Participation in Organizations*. Englewood Cliffs, NJ: Prentice Hall.

Vroom, V. H., & Yetton, P. W. (1973). *Leadership and decision-making*. Pittsburgh, PA: University of Pittsburgh Press.

Weber, M. (1947). *The theory of social and economic organization*. Glencoe, IL: Free Press.

Williams, S. (2018). Developing the capacity of culturally competent leaders to redress inequitable outcomes: Increasing opportunities for historically marginalized students. *Administrative Issues Journal: Education, Practice & Research*, *8*(1), 48–58.

Index

A, B, Cs, of strategic planning, 89–90, 92
accommodation, in management of conflict, 70, 72
active listening, 58, 62
aggressive communication, 61
assertive communication style, 58, 62
attitudes, 8–12, 14–16
attribution, 8, 11–12
avoidance, 70–72

behavioral view of leadership, 13, 20
bias, implicit and explicit, 9–10, 14, 49, 55, 73
Blanchard, R., 25–26, 30, 34
Bolman, L., 21–23
brainstorming, 49
Bryson, J., 89–90, 92

case study approach, xiv
change: agent, 16, 90, 95, 98, 100–102, 104–5; climate for, 96–97; evaluate, 104; institutionalize, 104–5; integrated approach, 95–96; operationalize, 103–4
classical theory, 1–2
collaboration in conflict management, 73
collaboration in negotiation, 80

collaborative strategic planning, 90–92
collective bargaining, 126
communication: effectiveness of, 58–61; external, 63–64; model and modes of, 57–58; significance of, 57
compromise, in management conflict, 70, 72
conflict resolution, 5, 72–73
contingency theory, 1, 3–5
control theory. *See* Glasser, W., control theory.
covenants, 102
cultural competency, 14–15

Deal, T., 21–23, 29
decision-making, 43–46
Delphi technique, 49–52
diagnostic approach, 11, 127, 132
diversity and inclusive practice, 46–47
Dweck, C., 33–34

empowering others, 78–79
empowerment, 112
ethical decision-making, 45–46
ethical issues, 78

feedback, value of, 63
force-field analysis, 100
forcing, 70, 73

Glasser, W., control theory, 36, 38
goal-setting theory, 39
group dynamic, 47
group decision-making, 44, 46–49
groupthink, 48, 52
growth mindset, 33–34, 118

halo effect, 9–10, 14
heart, 102, 109–11, 119–21. *See also* trust and respect
Hersey, P., 25–26

instructional. *See* leadership
interpersonal relations, 84, 102

Johari window, 59–60

leadership: behaviors, 23; effective formula of, 29; enacted, 110; frames of, 121; heart-led, 109–10; instructional model, 28; mindfulness in, 118–19; mission-centric, 27–28; servant, 23, 113–14; situational, 20–21, 23, 29, 67; through transition, 95; transformational, 26–27; transformational, emergence of, 30
learning process: behaviorist approach, 12; cognitive approach, 13; social approach, 13–14
Lewin, 100
locus of control, 12, 112

Maslow's theory, 36–38
matrix design, 64–65
mindfulness in. *See* leadership
mission-centric. *See* leadership
moral framing, 23
motivation, 33–34, 66, 98, 112, 118

National Association of Elementary School Principals (NAESP), 28
nominal group technique, 49–52

open systems theory, 3–5, 66
organizational: culture, 7–8; culture, process of, 8–11; structure, 2–5

perception, 8–9
perceptual distortions, 9
planning: process, 91, 95; strategic, 85–92; task force (PTF), 90–91
power, sources of: coercive, 80; expert, 80–81; legitimate/positional, 79; organizational, 79–80; personal, 80–81; referent, 80–81; reward, 79
power and dependence, 78
praise and reprimand, 34
projection, 10

redesign of work, 40
reinforcement theory, 35
reward systems. *See* praise and reprimand

Sanaghan, P., 89–92
self-fulfilling prophecy, 11–12
Simon, H., 47, 101
situational. *See* leadership
social systems theory, 1, 3–4, 66
stereotyping, 9
strategic planning. *See* planning

teamwork, 113
trait theory, 20
transformational. *See* leadership
trust and respect, 112

vision, educational, 30, 83
Vroom/Yetton model, 44–45, 67

About the Authors

Chris Heasley is an assistant professor of educational leadership in the School of Health Studies and Education at Saint Joseph's University, Philadelphia. Before teaching, he served more than eighteen years as a university administrator at both public and private institutions of higher education. He teaches courses on advanced quantitative research in education; educational leaders as researcher and reflective practitioner; and policy, politics, and community relations.

Robert Palestini has been an educator for more than fifty years, serving as a high school science teacher, principal, superintendent of schools, and university dean. He is currently dean emeritus and professor of educational leadership, as well as the founding executive director of the Educational Leadership Institute and Center for Catholic Urban Education at Saint Joseph's University.